PROMOTING AFRICAN ENTERPRISE

Promoting African Enterprise

BRUCE DINWIDDY

CROOM HELM LONDON
in association with
THE OVERSEAS DEVELOPMENT INSTITUTE

First published 1974
© 1974 by Overseas Development Institute

Croom Helm Ltd
2–10 St. John's Road London SW11

ISBN 0–85664–068–9

Printed and bound in Great Britain
by Redwood Burn Ltd, Trowbridge and Esher.

Contents

Foreword

In the first stage of the struggle for development, many developing countries placed inordinate emphasis on the early establishment of new industries, while neglecting the growth of agriculture – and, in my opinion, failing to recognise the groundwork needed for the long-term growth of industry itself. The balance between agriculture and industry is now being rectified, but too little thought is still being devoted to assessing the basic needs of a flourishing, self-supporting, self-renewing industrial and commercial economy. The provision of finance for industry is fine. Smoking chimneys are fine. But no country can regard itself as developed until its indigenous resources are capable of renewing and continuing the growth of its industry and commerce. One indispensable condition of economic independence is the manpower which will initiate and uphold new and constantly increasing numbers of enterprises. Any country which aims to become self-supporting must have an adequate reservoir of men who have the judgement, the initiative, the courage and the determination to conceive and launch new enterprises and of managers who run those enterprises and ensure that they are economically successful. This is just as true in countries where the Government wishes to monopolise industry or commerce as in those which favour private enterprise or a mixed economy.

Western Europe and North America evolved their tradition of entrepreneurship and their large class of enterprising businessmen over centuries, making mistakes, wasting resources and creating injustices and imbalances in the process. The developing countries, with their fast-growing populations, must do everything possible to telescope the process and reduce the errors. It must be conceded that, even with the benefit of Western experience, the process will be long; it will have small beginnings and will take time to bear significant fruit. Any work which can speed up the process deserves to be welcomed and carefully considered. Bruce Dinwiddy's study provides a useful survey of the problem as it exists in some parts of Africa and of some efforts which are being made towards meeting it, and makes some suggestions for further work. Having been commissioned by the Overseas Development Administration, it naturally has a strong slant towards providing guidance to the aid-giver, but it contains information which should be of broader interest to anyone concerned with African development.

I was Chairman of the working party that he mentions on page ix but our function was simply to help him choose the locale of his researches and the general scheme of his work. His findings and conclusions are entirely his own. The book provides a lucid birds-eye view of the subject and I recommend it to all who wish to see the new countries of Africa move towards an enduring and self-renewing industrial and commercial development.

B. Berkoff

Introduction

This book is the outcome of a study commissioned from ODI by the Overseas Development Administration at the end of 1970. The agreed terms of reference were as follows:

> The study will seek to establish the extent to which Africans have entered the private sector of commerce and industry as entrepreneurs, and will investigate means of promoting this process.
>
> After identifying some of the obstacles to successful entrepreneurship, the study will contain an analysis of:
>
> 1 Possible ways in which governments or other agencies (including private bodies) can assist and promote the development of entrepreneurship and small-scale industries.
> 2 The role that overseas aid might play in this, e.g. through technical assistance or financial aid.
> 3 Channels for the application of aid.
>
> In order to keep the study within manageable proportions it is intended that attention should be focussed on a selected group of African countries.

It was also agreed that the study would mainly concentrate on means to promote the further emergence of indigenous entrepreneurs and economic expansion of their activities, including the possible development of new channels for the application of external assistance.

The direct research has been the responsibility of the author, under general supervision of Robert Wood, ODI's Director of Studies. But broad strategy was worked out with the advice and assistance of a working party, drawn from government, business, and academic circles. Chaired by Ben Berkoff, the working party met five times during the course of the study; and although its members are in no way implicated in the statements and opinions contained in the report, the author is extremely grateful to them for their help and encouragement and particularly for their comments on an earlier draft.

The author wishes to thank, in addition to the chairman and members of the working party, all those who helped him with advice or information, including those who commented on the work when it was in draft. He is especially grateful for all the assistance and co-operation he received, from a great many sources, during his travels abroad.

Apart from the implicit exclusion of the state sector, and also of all agricultural activities, the terms of reference did not define the term 'entrepreneurship'. In practice, this has been taken to embrace any non-farming enterprise predominantly owned by Africans. In the more advanced countries of West Africa, African-owned enterprises already include fairly sophisticated manufacturing industries, whereas in the independent countries of Southern Africa there have, at least until very recently, been virtually no African-owned enterprises other than small retail stores. Furthermore, no attempt has been made to limit the study to Schumpeterian 'innovators': there can be no sharp distinction between those who genuinely introduce new ideas and new ways of doing things, and those who merely copy the style and practices of others. Briefly, then, the study concerns all private sector African businessmen except farmers; and, throughout this report, 'entrepreneur' and 'businessman' are interchangeable terms.

The study has largely been restricted to four countries: Ghana, Kenya, Malawi, and Swaziland. These countries were finally selected in August 1971 at the working party meeting which considered an interim report prepared after a first African field trip, lasting eight weeks, which also included brief visits to Uganda and Zambia. The author made a second trip to Africa, lasting seven weeks and merely covering the four main countries, in mid-1972; and he also twice visited the headquarters of ILO and UNIDO, in Geneva and Vienna respectively, to hold discussions with officials concerned in management and entre-preneurial training, and to consult relevant reports and documents which were not available in London.

Immediately following this Introduction there is a brief summary, largely based on the General Conclusions, of the study's main findings. The main body of the book is divided into two parts. Part I, which is mainly based on the four countries selected for detailed study but which also makes occasional reference to other parts of Africa, begins with a general appraisal of the present state of African entrepreneur-ship, an examination of government policies and attitudes towards the African private sector, and an outline of the characteristic problems faced by African businessmen. This is followed by a brief classification of the main types of business promotion programme which have been adopted, ostensibly at least, in order to assist African businessmen: and there is a short summary of the relevant assistance currently being given by external agencies. The next three chapters examine more closely, within the limits of available data, directly comparable measures which have been adopted in two or more of the four countries. If disproportionate space appears to have been given to methods of discrimination against established alien businessmen, this does at least reflect the main emphasis of recent programmes.

Part II consists of four separate country-studies. Each one first examines more closely, within the political and economic context of the country concerned, the present state of African enterprise. It then describes, and comments upon, past and present business promotion programmes, and a concluding section examines the scope for new or more effective programmes, and assesses the corresponding prospective role of external agencies.

Part I

Chapter 1 The Present Situation

The Present State of African Private Enterprise

In all African countries south of Sahara, most of the largest business enterprises are owned and controlled either by non-Africans or by the state. This is not to say that Africa has no indigenous entrepreneurial tradition: recent studies have emphasised that there is a long history of African trade, particularly in West Africa. During the nineteenth and early twentieth centuries, however, African private enterprise was largely overshadowed by the incursion of aliens — principally Europeans, Levantines, and Asians. In some countries, including Kenya and Swaziland, this even extended to the agricultural sector and the production of cash crops. In others, notably in West Africa, alien domination did not prevent the growth of some very substantial African traders. But outside agriculture (and the marketing of agricultural produce, which was often entrusted to State corporations), the modern private sector was almost everywhere developed principally by foreigners. State enterprises were largely restricted to the provision of basic services such as were becoming an accepted public responsibility within Europe.

In the late 1950s and the 1960s, therefore, Africa's newly-independent governments inherited economies whose commerce and industry was still heavily dominated by expatriates or aliens. It little mattered that around the time of independence many foreigners took African nationality. This process merely served to strengthen and perpetuate the non-African presence; and although most governments chose as their first priority the localisation of the civil service (and, in the case of grant-aided countries, the need to balance their annual recurrent budgets) and have only more recently turned their attention to the private sector, it is easy to understand why the politically independent should wish to lessen their continuing economic dependence on the entrepreneurship of essentially non-African people. Economic nationalism has been manifested, to varying extents in different countries, in the nationalisation of foreign enterprise and in special measures to assist indigenous enterprise. The latter area fairly new phenomenon, however; and in most countries the previous

3

non-African domination was so complete that, outside West Africa, there are still very few African-owned private businesses whose individual operations make a significant contribution to the national product.

Statistics about African enterprises are therefore very inadequate, and such as do exist have usually not been compiled on any comprehensive basis but reflect, rather, the needs of some specific government department or agency – concerned, for example, with issuing a particular type of licence. On the other hand, especially if one includes the hundreds of thousands of Africans, mainly farmers, who engage in some form of craft or service activity on a part-time basis, there are many more African businessmen, engaged in a fairly wide range of activities, than is generally recognised; and although the great majority of these smallest 'enterprises' are far beyond the reach of any programme conceived to assist African businessmen directly, it should be appreciated that they fulfil a crucial function in bridging the 'gap' between the traditional and modern sectors. This ill-defined area, where the cash and barter economies meet, has been largely excluded from the present study; but it can hardly be emphasised too strongly that government policies and regulations should at least be conducive to the existence of these very small entrepreneurial activities, which are important both in themselves, as breeding grounds for larger-scale entrepreneurship, and also because, particularly in the rural areas, they can make a vital contribution to improved living standards – among subsistence farmers, for whom they provide an incentive for cash crop production, as well as among the entrepreneurs themselves.

The scale and scope of larger entrepreneurship varies very greatly in different parts of Africa: if one likens the present state of African entrepreneurship to a spectrum, Ghana is near one end, Malawi and Swaziland are near the other, and Kenya is roughly in the middle. Among English-speaking countries, Ghana and (even more so) Nigeria both possess significant numbers of African businessmen, characteristically owning two or three separate businesses, who individually employ a total of a hundred or more people, while it is unusual in Malawi and Swaziland to find an African business with as many as ten employees. The range of African entrepreneurship is correspondingly wider in West Africa: some West Africans own quite sophisticated industries, making textiles, processed foods, or suitcases, for example, whereas, in independent Southern Africa, African-owned manufacturing enterprises are still very rare. The most common form of African enterprises, in all the countries included in this study, is shop-keeping;

but in addition to the other African-owned enterprises, such as bars and tailoring establishments commonly situated in trading centres, all the countries have indigenous contractors and transport operators. The largest of these tend, again, to be found in West Africa; and just because the spectrum of current entrepreneurial development is so broad, government efforts to promote entrepreneurship must be directed, in different countries, at very different sorts of businessmen. For example, African businessmen who might be considered fairly large in Malawi would very probably be ignored, as insignificantly small, in Ghana.

Government Policies towards African Private Sector Development

In order to see African business promotion programmes in their proper context, it is important first to examine the basic motivation of such programmes: in seeking to promote indigenous enterprise, African governments are usually more concerned merely to increase the degree of active African participation, than to accomplish any overall economic improvement such as faster growth or increased employment. It should also be remembered that the encouragement of the indigenous private sector is only one means towards Africanisation: most African governments have also sought to promote African participation through 'localisation' of the personnel of expatriate companies and through the direct expansion of the public sector.

Expansion of the public sector — whether this be through the nationalisation of existing private businesses, the formation of joint ventures, or the establishment of new state enterprises — may have a purely socialist motivation; and some African governments, notably those of Tanzania and Zambia, have made it clear that they would not tolerate Western-style capitalism indefinitely even if the individual capitalists were Africans. Most governments have been less outspoken; but it does seem probable that, to the political and administrative elites of at least the majority of English-speaking African countries, wider public ownership (though they cannot always afford it) seems preferable to the sort of balance of power, between public and private interests, which is widely accepted in advanced Western countries. It may be that African governments will more readily accept the existence of an independent business sector if and when this is subject to greater local control; and that, despite a continuing reliance on foreign capital and expertise, they will, for example, be relatively satisfied once expatriate managers are replaced by Africans. Generally, however, and although some countries such as Kenya and Swaziland may prove to be exceptions, the nationalistic aspirations of African governments at present seem to extend rather further than this. It remains to be seen whether political experience will induce governments to tolerate the growth of a substantial, politically independent, African middle class. In any case, it must be accepted for the purposes of this study that Africanisation, of whatever sort, is a legitimate medium-term social objective, even though it may sometimes involve a short-term economic loss; and also, particularly in view of the administrative bottlenecks which already exist in most countries, severely prejudicing the efficiency of established state enterprises, that the widespread development of an African private sector may be an essential condition for new job opportunities and general improvements in African standards of living. Even Zambia has a programme (operated by Rucom Industries, a wholly-owned subsidiary of the state holding company Indeco) for the encouragement of new African private enterprise in rural areas.

The ambivalence of government attitudes is also manifested in some of the programmes ostensibly intended directly to assist African businessmen. This is especially true where national trading corporations are concerned: although usually these have initially been conceived in the interests of small African traders, to circumvent the alien domination of wholesaling, they easily acquire an institutional momentum of their own which makes them more interested in their own future. In both Ghana and Kenya, the respective governments seem to be unworried by the prospect (already becoming a reality in Ghana) that their national trading corporations may actually compete with the African private sector, and inhibit the latter's development.

Problems of African Businessmen

There are other, more general, respects in which government policies, and the way in which they are administered, can be a substantial hindrance to African businessmen. These will be reviewed at the end of this section, which will be concerned, first, to outline the various problems which are more directly associated with the characteristics of African businessmen themselves – particularly with their motivation, their social environment, their individual capacity and experience, and their collective reputation.

The most obvious internal constraint to the development of African private enterprise lies in the local traditions of many African peoples.

Most notably in the independent countries of East and Southern Africa – where, compared to West Africa, contact with Western societies has been fairly recent – there are still relatively few indigenous 'entrepreneurs', at least in the sense in which Europeans use the term. Even in tribes (such as the Kikuyu in Kenya) which have some entrepreneurial tradition, this developed over a period and usually covered a rather limited field (trading, fishing, or cattle-farming, for example). Such entrepreneurship as does exist in Africa has thus been largely imitative rather than innovative; and although some exceptional entrepreneurs have been very successful, many of these have gone into business only because of their lack of formal education, and their consequent effective exclusion from more secure and prestigious forms of employment.

The sociological background to African entrepreneurship is an enormous subject; and since this is also an area where generalisation can be particularly misleading – even (because of tribal differences) where this is confined to specific countries – it has not been possible to treat it adequately in the present study. Nevertheless, on the assumption that the development of entrepreneurial initiative will make it easier for Africans to come to terms with the modern world, it must be asked whether existing systems of education and training are serving Africa's needs. And the fact that a child's outlook and approach to life depends fundamentally on home upbringing rather than on school merely emphasises the length of time-scale involved: for home environment is heavily conditioned by the experience – in the broadest sense – of the parents themselves. African educational systems, having been introduced by Missions, were mainly concerned with literacy and religious instruction, and developed, as colonial governments took an increasing share of the responsibility, primarily to support the localisation and expansion of the public service. School curricula and teaching methods are admittedly now being given a more practical orientation in most countries; but even these advances may not significantly accelerate the emergence of an independent entrepreneurial class. Merely to improve facilities for technical and vocational education is not enough. Both within schools and at specialised training institutions, such education is primarily designed to serve the needs of governments, parastatals, and large expatriate companies. Although, as a result of various government policies, these employers offer the greatest material rewards, prospective entrepreneurs need to be motivated towards *self*-employment, which needs to be looked upon as something better than an undesirable last resort.

Even the practising African entrepreneur is usually inhibited by a passively hostile social environment. In this regard, it is interesting that many of the more successful African businessmen have broadened their horizons by foreign travel, or at least by working fairly closely (within an expatriate company or a government agency) with Europeans. In West Africa, where businessmen are generally better educated and longer established than their counterparts elsewhere, many have been to Europe, while the larger businessmen in Malawi and Swaziland have usually spent some time in Rhodesia or South Africa.

Experience abroad (which itself witnesses to entrepreneurial initiative in the person who seeks it) does serve to show how other societies are organised, and to reveal possible business opportunities which might be exploited at home. But, after return, even the Ghanaian 'been-to' (a term reserved for those who have been overseas) finds it virtually impossible to avoid increasing family responsibilities and commitments as his business expands. The African extended family (the basis of an extensive social security system) is, of course, a drain on the successful politician or civil servant as well as on the successful businessman; but whereas any paid employee has a relatively fixed salary, which he cannot consistently overspend, the independent businessman continually faces the danger (exacerbated by the fact that his accounting system, such as it is, may not disclose what is happening) that he may draw not only on his profits (thus limiting his capacity to re-invest) but also on his accumulated capital assets. African businessmen are directly constrained by their own managerial inadequacies (discussed below); but quite apart from these, it may be entirely rational, given their difficulty in retaining profits for expansion (and also, in some countries, the recurring vicissitudes of the business climate), for African businessmen to diversify into more secure investments such as land and housing. Peter Garlick found, in Ghana, that a major objective of African traders was to establish other sources of income and thus 'to provide for immediate and future personal and family needs, particularly by means of the acquisition of real property'.[1]

The conventional analyses of the other problems facing indigenous entrepreneurs in different African countries are strikingly similar. Basically, these are seen to be the difficulty of raising capital and obtaining credit, the lack of appropriate knowledge, experience, and skills, and the presence (at least until recently) of non-African competition. The first two of these, the financial and the intrinsically personal problems characteristic of African businessmen, interact. Thus, at all levels and in all countries, the lack of commercial and technical expertise, together with the collective reputation of Africans for being slow to service and repay their debts, makes it difficult for the African businessman to obtain either loans or credit through the usual banking or trade channels. Individual businessmen tend to think that the fundamental constraint is lack of finance; and there are undoubtedly some who would indeed be able to put additional capital to profitable use. But no African government yet seems to have attained any proficiency in identifying these, and even in Nigeria, where their number might be expected to be relatively large, S.P. Schatz, having identified the high cost of operating government loans schemes, was driven to conclude that the country's resources might be put to better use through diversion 'to other business-assistance programmes'.[2]

The internal management problems of African businessmen vary, of course, according to the nature of the business concerned; and technical incapacities obviously loom relatively large in small industries and in the provision of specialised services (ranging from shoe-repair to panel-beating and electrical contracting). All African businessmen, however, as their businesses grow to any size, tend to meet a ceiling where their desire to maintain direct supervision over every aspect of their business, their failure to delegate any significant responsibilities to subordinates (even to the extent of setting up a more impersonal record-keeping system) and their reluctance to form partnerships or co-operatives with fellow-Africans, effectively limit their further expansion. They also come under increasing personal stress; and if, as often happens, they diversify into other business activities (partly in order to spread their risks but also because they instinctively feel that it will be easier to keep strict personal control over two or three small businesses rather than one larger one), this only worsens their predicament. It is at this stage (which in Southern African countries has so far rarely been reached, since it only occurs when total employees number about thirty to fifty people), that the African businessman may meet his worst financial crisis; but it is not peculiar to African businessmen that when they seem in greatest need of more money they often also urgently need to review their system of management. It will be a recurring theme, throughout this report, that financial assistance cannot in itself provide a solution to African business problems, and that an essential feature of any business promotion programme must be a conscious attempt to identify and counteract the inherent, personal constraints to African entrepreneurial development.

African governments have recognised, as has already been observed, that the development of entrepreneurship has also been severely limited by the continued existence of alien business communities which became firmly entrenched during the colonial period. The largest companies have usually been established and operated by Europeans; but African businessmen have so far been more directly affected by competition from smaller concerns, mainly run by Levantines in West Africa and by Asians in East and Southern Africa. This alien domination has been particularly marked in East Africa, Zambia, and Malawi; for there have been proportionally more Asians than Levantines and the Asian commercial structure, based on caste and kinship, has been intensely self-centred. Marris and Somerset wrote of Kenya's Indian immigrants that:

> Though they pioneered shopkeeping far into the African country-side, they remained apart, jealously guarding for their family and friends the opportunities they had sought out. In time they have come to be deeply resented. They are now politically too insecure and socially too self-enclosed to exploit the opportunities of an African state. As intermediaries between the small-scale, rural economy and the international economy which contains it, they can only give way to Africans.[3]

None the less, concrete government action has been required in order to break into the Asian monopoly; and this in itself has not enabled Africans to take over where Asians left off. Quite apart from their managerial inexperience, Africans have to establish their own external business relationships — with their suppliers, with their customers, with commercial banks, and with one another. The extent to which this may be a problem varies, again, in proportion to the scale and nature of the business concerned, and according to the location of its market. But every African businessman has to establish a working relationship with his government (or perhaps with several different government agencies); and it is ironic that this is often a particularly difficult task.

It is probably no exaggeration to say that in some African countries the greatest single constraint on indigenous entrepreneurship is uncertainty with regard to government policy and intentions.[4] Certainly, in Ghana indigenous entrepreneurs have suffered — with the rest of the private sector — from repeated changes in successive governments' economic policy. In other countries, with less experienced civil servants, African businessmen may have suffered rather more from administrative inefficiencies and bottlenecks. But everywhere the larger businessmen have to grapple with complicated licensing procedures (especially for imports) and with what they consider to be unreasonably strict requirements concerning, for example, minimum wages and other conditions of employment; and even the smallest are often hampered by petty regulations which can only be tolerated because they are not usually enforced. Governments genuinely seeking to promote African entrepreneurial development probably need to pay closer attention to improving the general business environment, in particular by removing unnecessary restrictions to business activity, rather than to selecting individual entrepreneurs for special assistance.

Governments also need to improve their public relations. At present there is widespread antipathy between bureaucrats and businessmen, with civil servants taking an attitude which is often disparaging and which tends even at its best to be rather patronising, while businessmen, for their part, regard the civil service with distrust and probably, in most cases, not a little jealousy. This makes for a climate which is conducive neither to spontaneous entrepreneurial development nor to the design and implementation of successful business promotion programmes.

Notes

1. P.C. Garlick, *African Traders and Economic Development in Ghana*, Oxford University Press, London, 1971.
2. S.P. Schatz, 'The High Cost of Aiding Business in Developing Economies: Nigeria's Loans Programmes', *Oxford Economic Papers*, Nov. 1968.
3. Peter Marris and Anthony Somerset, *African Businessmen*, Routledge and Kegan Paul, 1971, p.6.
4. See, for example, K.A. Hameed's unpublished thesis on entrepreneurship in the Sudan, *Some Aspects of the Emergence of Entrepreneurship in a Newly Independent Country*, submitted to Oxford University in September 1969.

Chapter 2 Business Promotion Programmes : a Classification

A fairly wide range of measures and programmes have been adopted by African governments, and by other agencies, with the explicit object of assisting African businessmen. Many of these have also served other purposes: the 1972 deportation of Uganda's non-citizen Asians was motivated at least as much by political or racial prejudice as by a desire to foster indigenous enterprise, and there are many less extreme examples of programmes or institutions which make some partial contribution to African business development without this being their prime objective. This chapter groups all types of 'programme' together and classifies them according to their general function rather than their direct relevance to African entrepreneurship. It should also be noted that the classification is mainly based on the past and present experience of just four countries – Ghana, Kenya, Malawi, and Swaziland. A more comprehensive account, of the range of promotional measures adopted in some seventeen African countries, may be found in the unpublished report prepared by J.C. de Wilde for the World Bank.[1] The measures are here grouped under four main headings; in order to avoid unnecessary repetition, relatively less space is given to types of programme which are considered in greater detail in the following three chapters. A concluding section examines the present role, in this field, of foreign governments and other external agencies.

Discrimination

The greatest impact on the African business environment has been made, at least in Ghana, Kenya, and Malawi, by discriminatory measures against aliens. (These were essentially *counter*-discriminatory, in the sense that they merely offset the long-established and otherwise self-perpetuating dominance of small business by closely-knit alien communities.) Discrimination has characteristically been achieved through legal or administrative action to reserve certain business sectors or geographical areas exclusively for African (or citizen) businessmen. In addition, individual aliens have in some countries had their licences withdrawn on an apparently more random basis; and discrimination has also been practised by national trading corporations established, at least in part, specifically for this purpose. National trading corporations are usually intended at least to cover their costs, so that, except for some relatively small administrative costs, discrimination should generally not involve governments in much direct expense. It will be argued in Chapter 3 that discrimination against non-Africans may be an important precondition to African business development. In any case, especially in view of its undoubted political popularity, it is not hard to see why it should have been so widely practised.

Finance

Other government efforts to assist African businessmen have historically tended to concentrate on providing capital finance. This has largely been in response to the difficulties experienced by Africans in obtaining loans or credit through the usual channels: commercial banks, most of them still expatriate-controlled and able to rely mainly on larger-scale government and expatriate business, know from their limited experience that African businessmen are a poor risk, and they are correspondingly reluctant (or, because of accelerated localisation, actually unable) to afford the specialised staff which would be required to increase their African lending. While expatriate suppliers and distributors, though these increasingly rely on African traders to sell their goods and therefore do have an obvious interest in building up their African business, are equally wary with regard to giving credit. Most commonly, governments have operated formal business loan schemes, such as are discussed in Chapter 4; but various other means have been adopted for providing principally medium- and short-term assistance to African businessmen. These have included the provision of trade credit through national trading corporations (see Chapter 3), Swaziland's hire purchase scheme for machinery and equipment (Chapter 5), and, in Ghana, a scheme for the official guarantee of commercial bank credit. (Ghana's credit guarantee scheme is described in some detail in Chapter 6.) Despite its particular shortcomings, it is a characteristic advantage of any credit guarantee scheme that it does help to integrate African businessmen within the broader business community. On the other hand, unless there is some responsible agency to help identify promising entrepreneurs, a credit guarantee scheme cannot succeed (at least without substantial cost to the government) until a sufficient number of local businessmen have attained a minimum level of sophistication and experience.

Training

In all the four countries, there are a range of government institutions which provide technical, managerial or vocational training. But these, as was pointed out in Chapter 1, have mainly been designed to serve the needs of governments, public corporations, and expatriate companies. Among institutions offering full-time courses, only the Kenya Industrial Training Institute and Kenya's Village Polytechnics explicitly aim to prepare their trainees for self-employment; but quite a few bodies do offer occasional or part-time training and assistance to practising African businessmen. The ILO-sponsored management training centres in Ghana and Kenya both now make some specific provision for entrepreneurial training or advice; and it may be added that Uganda's Management Training and Advisory Centre, right from its foundation in 1966, aimed as one of its principal objectives 'to help citizens of Uganda to become entrepreneurs, by providing them with advisory services and instruction in simple management practices, particularly management accounting and marketing, technological guidance and practical demonstration'.

Uganda's Management Training Centre was the first in Africa to incorporate in its courses the McLelland techniques of 'achievement motivation training', aimed at developing more progressive and enterprising attitudes. The Centre's Staff claimed in 1971 that, of self-employed Ugandans who had been subjected to such training at small enterprises development courses, 80 percent had subsequently performed at a higher (i.e. more enterprising) level than would otherwise have been predicted of them; and, irrespective of the exact reliability of this figure, it does seem that where human attitudes are a significant limiting factor on entrepreneurial development, achievement motivation training – especially if it is integrated with more practical assistance – can yield substantial benefits.

On the general subject of courses, it should be added that, in themselves, these at present appear to be a totally inadequate means of business promotion. There are institutions, in all the four countries with which we are mainly concerned, which have run courses for African businessmen on an occasional, if not a regular, basis. But, quite apart from the problem of attracting people to attend such courses, the African businessman's education has typically not been sufficient to enable him to transfer concepts from one situation (the classroom) to another (his business). Some follow-up is also necessary, in order to help him to apply the teaching to his own individual problems.

Co-ordinated Business Promotion

In most countries, some of those who deal with African business promotion are moving towards the view that even where a specific group of businessmen is concerned (whether they be traders, building contractors, or small manufacturers) it is an illusion to hope that their performance can be dramatically improved by a narrow approach which concentrates on only one of the constraints discussed in the previous chapter. Rather, a realistic business promotion programme needs to offer or co-ordinate a whole range of inputs and services, including various forms of technical and managerial assistance or consultancy as well as (perhaps) some measures of discrimination against non-Africans and (probably, but only when the individual is capable of benefiting from it) finance. It must also be able, in as catalytic a fashion as possible, to help identify promising areas of entrepreneurial activity, and to advise on the planning and implementation of particular projects — whether they involve the expansion of existing businesses or the establishment of new ones.

Several francophone countries (as de Wilde has described) have established official agencies with a more or less general mandate to promote indigenous private enterprise. However, by 1972, of the four anglophone countries included in the present study, only Swaziland had attempted to introduce a really comprehensive programme (although a substantial streamlining and improvement of African business promotion was also understood to be under discussion in Kenya). Swaziland's Small Enterprises Promotion Office, and its associated companies, were designed to encourage all types of non-agricultural Swazi entrepreneurship; but, although this was an administratively economical approach in such a small country, it may be equally satisfactory (or even essential) in a larger country, for sectoral responsibilities to be more widely delegated to specialised agencies. In particular, there are obvious reasons for distinguishing the promotion of commerce and industry — since the latter requires a larger technical input and is also usually not so dependent on a geographically concentrated local market. If the government concerned can afford it, there are even clearly identifiable advantages to grouping African industries together in special estates; and this method of promotion, which is being practised in both Kenya and Swaziland, is discussed in Chapter 5.

On the other hand, a broader and more flexible approach may be adopted through the recruitment and training of a special cadre of business extension officers; and only Swaziland (whose small size has again been an undoubted advantage, particularly in terms of the country's access to relatively large amounts of external assistance) has introduced an extension service, manned in mid-1972 by one local officer and four expatriate volunteers and concentrating on traders, which has been able to reach a significant proportion of the country's entrepreneurs. Two other programmes – Ghana's Business Bureau and Partnership for Productivity's pilot project in Kenya – are probably of greater relevance to African business promotion generally. These give assistance to all sorts of African businessmen; and it is significant that both of them, in addition to being heavily dependent on external support (particularly in the form of expatriate personnel), have also found it necessary to concentrate on relatively small numbers of entrepreneurs. In mid-1972 Partnership for Productivity, with six expatriates and two senior local staff together covering about eighteen enterprises, was in fact much more intensively concentrated than the Ghana Business Bureau, whose three expatriates and four counterparts at Kumasi offered regular assistance to some sixty to seventy enterprises. But this partly resulted from the very different environments in which they were respectively operating: the Kumasi branch of the Business Bureau is based in Ghana's second largest industrial and commercial centre, while Partnership for Productivity has been attempting to develop entrepreneurship in what is, compared to Kumasi, a very backward area, centred on a small rural town. Furthermore, Partnership for Productivity has been involved in a number of other community development projects not directly related to business extension.

Ghana's Business Bureau and the Partnership for Productivity project are both essentially small and experimental; and neither Ghana (although it has an 'Office of Business Promotion') nor Kenya has a single government agency with specific overall responsibility for entrepreneurial development. However, there was the prospect in mid-1972 that a better coordinated approach might soon be adopted in Kenya by reviewing and redefining the functions of the Industrial and Commercial Development Corporation. In Malawi, although there was effectively no other organisation involved apart from the Import and

Export Company, this agency was not yet in a position to mount a comprehensive programme.

External Agencies

External agencies have so far not been widely involved in assisting African entrepreneurial development, and their individual commitments have generally been fairly small. Projects, in each of the four countries, which were directly concerned with entrepreneurship and which in mid-1972 were receiving external assistance, are listed in Table 1 (which needs to be read in conjunction with Chapters 6–9). It will be seen that although eight bilateral donors and one multilateral agency (the International Labour Office) were all supporting at least one project in Kenya, only Britain, the United States, West Germany and the ILO were supporting projects in other countries.

There are other external agencies which can play a valuable but less direct role in assisting African entrepreneurship. For example, the management training centre at Turin is used by the ILO for the overseas training of counterparts from its projects in Ghana and Kenya, while the Research Institute for Management Science, at Delft, runs six-month courses in the management of small-scale industries which have been attended by participants from more than sixty developing countries and which can be expected – at least in the future – to be used in the training of managers for indigenous African industries.

Britain's Intermediate Technology Development Group (ITDG) is also potentially of great importance to the development of technologies (e.g. for construction and small industry) which are more labour-intensive than modern Western technologies and which, since they have a smaller capital cost, indigenous entrepreneurs can more easily afford. ITDG, a private agency receiving some government support, is concerned with a much wider range of technologies than those directly relevant to this study. But the Group's Building for Development project has already helped Kenya's National Construction Corporation to design training programmes suitable for African contractors; another ITDG subsidiary, Inter-Technology Services, has undertaken consultancy work in Botswana, Lesotho and Swaziland; and the Group may become more closely associated, on a regular basis, with the small enterprises development programmes in both Swaziland and Botswana.

Apart from official and voluntary agencies, expatriate commercial bodies have an important bearing on African entrepreneurial

Table 1

External assistance to entrepreneurial development (1972)

	Ghana	Kenya	Malawi	Swaziland
Denmark				
West Germany		3 RIDCs (fa/ta)	RTSS (Fa/ta)	
India		KIE (fa/ta)		
Japan		KIE (fa)		
Norway		KITI (fa/ta)		
		RIDC (fa/ta)		
		NCC (fa/ta)		
Sweden				SEDCO (fa)
				2 IVS volunteers
UK		KIE (prospective fa/ta)		6 PC volunteers
		PfP (private support, incl. 1 volunteer)		
US	GBB (5 PC volunteers)	PfP (fa & private support)		
ILO	MDPI (ta)	MTAC (ta)		SEPO (ta)

Key: fa—financial aid
ta—technical assistance

GBB	Ghana Business Bureau	NCC	National Construction Corporation
IVS	International Voluntary Service	PC	Peace Corps
KIE	Kenya Industrial Estates	PfP	Partnership for Productivity
KITI	Kenya Industrial Training Institute	RIDC	Rural Industrial Development Centre
MDPI	Management Development and Productivity Institute	RTSS	Rural Trade School, Salima
		SEDCO	Small Enterprises Development Company
MTAC	Management Training and Advisory Centre	SEPO	Small Enterprises Promotion Offices

development. In particular, it is widely supposed within Africa that expatriate banks could play a larger role; but, as was pointed out earlier in this chapter, commercial banks have little incentive to seek out new African business. Other expatriate companies will also not expand their African credit, if they do not consider this to be in their commercial interest: on the other hand, African governments might themselves take a more enterprising attitude towards encouraging expatriate companies to purchase locally-produced goods and services. Generally, although foreign-owned industries and importers increasingly rely on African traders to distribute their goods and may therefore further increase the resources devoted to training and extension, the expatriate private sector cannot be expected, in its dealings with African businessmen, to do more than seems sensible in its own long-term interest.

Notes

1. *The Development of African Private Enterprise* IBRD/IDA, Dec. 1971.

Chapter 3 Methods of Discrimination

The Rationale of Discriminatory Policies

All African business promotion programmes involve, at least implicitly, some degree of discrimination against non-African businessmen. The present chapter is concerned with comparing measures which have been adopted, in each of the four countries, specifically in order to reduce the alien domination of the small business sector.

In large part, these initial attempts to localise the private sector have been a logical extension of the principles underlying the localisation of the civil service. They have been politically inspired; and although the bureaucracies which have implemented them may have had only a half-hearted commitment towards private sector development *per se*, these, like their political masters, have been more than willing, in the interests of consolidating national independence, to reduce or eliminate the alien business presence. It should be repeated, in order to define the political context of African business development more clearly, that most African governments may in fact not feel properly independent until they have also taken further steps to localise large-scale expatriate businesses as well.

Discrimination against smaller non-African businesses has usually been effected through licensing policies or through the operations of national trading corporations; and it is characteristic of both these forms of assistance that they have been neither concerned nor suited, at least in the short term, to boost overall levels of economic activity. Rather, they have sought to improve the African business environment at the direct expense of existing alien businesses: the acceleration of economic growth, or the provision of opportunities for employment, have at best been subsidiary objectives. African employment levels have obviously benefited, and overall employment may also have tended to increase. Moreover, it may reasonably be contended that wider African ownership was, and is still, an important pre-requisite for sustained economic development in the longer term. More immediately, however, most governments, although they have not explicitly acknowledged the fact, have been prepared to accept a socio-political trade-off between greater local control and reduced economic growth.

Discriminatory Licensing Policies

Three of the four countries have discriminated against non-Africans in the issue or renewal of business licences. It may be added that similar discriminatory policies have been very widely adopted elsewhere in sub-Saharan Africa; and although in one or two countries, notably Tanzania, they have ostensibly been motivated by socialism rather than nationalism, the main brunt has always been borne by non-Africans. In 1973, the only English-speaking independent African countries where no overtly discriminatory licensing policies have yet been initiated are Botswana, Lesotho, and Swaziland, where no readily identifiable, small business communities exist, and whose governments would probably be reluctant to discriminate against small European businesses because of the adverse effect this would have on the general climate for foreign investment. So far as Ghana, Kenya and Malawi are concerned, there is a broad distinction – at least in degree – between Ghana's universal reservation to local citizens of certain strictly defined business sectors, and the more limited geographical restrictions (applied to a narrower range of businesses, but supported by arbitrary delicensing of particular individuals) introduced in Kenya and Malawi.

The Ghanaian Business (Promotion) Act, passed in July 1970, superseded the Ghanaian Enterprises Decree, published by the National Liberation Council in December 1968. The latter laid down a five-year timetable for the exclusion of non-Ghanaians (principally Lebanese, Indians, and Nigerians) from a wide range of 'small-scale' commercial and industrial enterprises, but had never been made properly effective. Under the Act, it was explicitly stated that with effect from 1 August 1970 no alien was to engage in retail or wholesale trade whose annual sales (as declared in his 1967/68 tax return) did not exceed ₡500,000, and also that with effect from the same date all alien participation was to be excluded from enterprises concerned with overseas business representation, taxi services, and the hire-purchase sale of taxis. It was further laid down that as from 30 June 1971 aliens were not to engage in commercial transportation by land, nor in bakery, printing, beauty culture, produce brokerage, advertising and publicity, or manufacture of cement blocks for sale. It was emphasised that there was still room for foreign participation in the economy: the Act was intended merely to reserve certain sectors of the economy to Ghanaians and (by the process of elimination) 'to clarify the future role of foreign businesses'. The Act also provided for the establishment of a Ghanaian Enterprises Advisory Committee, whose main function was to advise the Government on appropriate policies for the promotion of Ghanaian enterprise: the Committee had no executive powers, it met only a few times, and it appears to have had little influence on government policy.

Although the 1970 Act seems to have been something of a leap in the dark, it appears to have been fairly successful. A few exceptions were allowed (for example, the United Africa Company was allowed to maintain its own advertising agency); a significant but unknown number of businesses were run by Lebanese who already had Ghanaian nationality and who were therefore not affected; and there can be no doubt that there are many cases of companies which, although they have nominally changed hands, are still controlled by their former owners. Nevertheless, the Act has accelerated the transfer to Ghanaians of businesses with which they had for the most part become well able to cope, and there do not seem to have been significant ill-effects (though these might in any case have been obscured by other economic changes) in terms of disruption of local markets or services. The Bank of Ghana's scheme for the guarantee of commercial bank credit (introduced in December 1969), together with the special small business loans scheme (1970), played some part in facilitating Ghanaian access to capital; but more important, there were by 1970 sufficient numbers of Ghanaians with appropriate education, background and resources, for the government's optimism to be justified. Individual transfers were left almost entirely to private treaty. The Office of Business Promotion, established in 1970 as a special unit within the Ministry of Finance and Economic Planning, was intended to advise and assist Ghanaians with regard to any problems connected with purchase; but it was inadequately staffed and was unable to take any significant role. Although it was officially estimated in August 1970 that a total of about 600 alien enterprises, with a total turnover of ₵15m, would be affected, it is not possible to estimate either the total amount of money which was mobilised for the purchase of such businesses, or the extent to which Ghanaian purchasers relied on money made available through the credit guarantee scheme or the small business loan scheme.

In Kenya, where the Asian business community has been much larger than the alien community in Ghana, the government took the first steps towards discrimination against non-Kenyan businesses in 1967. The Trade Licensing Act of that year provides for the licensing of wholesale and retail trade, import and export trade, commission agencies, indent agencies, manufacturers' representatives, produce dealers and brokers, business brokers and management consultants, insurance and estate agents, launderers and dry cleaners, hairdressers, and motor vehicle repairers. The government was empowered to specify particular areas of cities and towns as general trading areas where both citizens and non-citizens could be licensed to operate; and elsewhere (except where a non-citizen was given specific authority, written into his licence) licences were only to be issued to citizens. Six such areas have been delineated – in Nairobi, Mombasa, Kisumu, Nakuru, Eldoret, and Thika – and some of these have been reduced in size since their boundaries were first drawn. In addition, government was empowered to specify goods which could be marketed only by Kenya citizens; the list of such goods, which has several times been extended, contains some fifty items including maize and maize meal, sugar, meat, soap, matches, soft drinks, blankets, shoes and sandals, bicycles, shovels and spades, and cement.

Irrespective of the boundaries of the general trading areas, further delicensing of non-citizens has been enforced on an *ad hoc* basis. Non-citizen businessmen are required to renew their licences annually; and the government has published lists of non-citizen businesses whose licences would not be renewed after certain dates. On 10 May 1972, for example, it was announced by the Minister of Commerce and Industry that, 'in pursuance of the government's policy of placing the economy of this country into the hands of local citizens', 300 named companies, owned by non-citizens, were to be taken over by citizens by 1 October.

Compared to Ghana, the localisation of non-citizen businesses in Kenya has been more closely planned and overseen by the government. But a larger number of businesses is involved, and because the Asian community (including Kenya citizens) is so large, it has been difficult to ensure that the implicit objective of the exercise (i.e. to increase the share of *African* Kenyans in the small business sector) was achieved. The government estimates that, at the end of 1970, 668 businesses formerly owned by non-citizens, with a total turnover at the time of transfer of K£21m, had been transferred to citizens. The Industrial and Commercial Development Corporation's small business loans schemes have contributed a significant part of the capital necessary for African purchase: in June 1971 nearly K£3m was outstanding to the Corporation from borrowers under its small commercial and business property loans schemes, and most of this money had probably been employed in the purchase of alien businesses. Substantial amounts must also have been raised privately; but it should be added that no estimate is available, with respect to those businesses which had changed hands by December 1970, of the proportion which had in fact been transferred to Africans. As in Ghana, there have undoubtedly been many 'transfers' which nevertheless left effective ownership and control in non-citizen hands; but the government has made determined efforts to reduce this sort of evasion, and transfers have to be approved by special District Trade Licensing Committees, chaired by District Commissioners.

By mid-1972, Kenya's rural areas and smaller District centres contained very few non-citizen traders, but it will be some time before Africans can acquire sufficient capital and experience to take over all the non-citizen business in the larger towns. Although the effective bottleneck is generally thought to be shortage of capital (despite the ICDC's small business loan scheme and the considerable amounts which have also been mobilised from purely private sources), the more fundamental constraints continue to be management inexperience and the absence of real integration into the trading community of African traders and those non-Africans who, as citizens, are untouched by the Trade Licensing Act. Irrespective of whether enough money is available for purchase, the distribution system – which so far has held up quite well – would certainly suffer if the government tried unduly to accelerate the rate of Africanisation; and it is more important that improved follow-up, in terms of practical advice, should be provided to those businesses which have already been taken over.

The Africanisation programme in Malawi has so far been considerably less extensive than in either Ghana or Kenya. But at present there is a much greater dearth of Africans with the necessary potential to take over alien businesses. Even the limited measures already taken have led to a significant deterioration in the standard of rural distribution services.

The government's policy of localisation was first announced in 1968. With effect from the beginning of 1969, the issue and renewal of all non-Malawian trading licences was centralised in the Ministry of Trade and Industry; and as from 1 July 1970, no non-Malawians were permitted to trade in rural areas. Unlike Kenya, Malawi has very few non-African citizens, and although no estimate is available concerning the total number of businesses which have been affected, it has been relatively easy to ensure that localisation took place. On the other hand, this ease of administration also prevented the sorts of evasion which in Kenya served to cushion the immediate economic effects: the Government's 1972 Economic Report noted that 'Changes in trading arrangements, especially in the rural areas, combined with some transport shortages, meant that growth in retail and distributive services to the public did not expand in line with demand'.[1] Although by 1972 some Malawians, relieved of Asian competition, were achieving an excellent trade, a number of formerly Asian-operated premises had merely closed down, while others housed businesses carrying a much reduced range of stock.

Following its abortive partnership with Bookers (Malawi) in the National Trading Corporation (see Chapter 8), in mid-1972 the government was hoping to improve the system of rural distribution through the efforts of the wholly state-owned Import and Export Company (see below p.26). Despite pressures from the African Business-men's Association, the government appeared to have no plans for any wider general withdrawal of non-Malawian licences, but there continued to be a certain amount of *ad hoc* delicensing of individuals. And although the government claimed that licences in unrestricted areas were never withdrawn except for good reason (e.g. over-charging, or the illicit export of foreign exchange), it seemed that continuing uncer-tainty among Asian traders still caused them to delay refurbishing their stocks in the first four months of each year, while they waited to hear whether their licences would be renewed.

Discriminatory licensing policies, such as those which have been described, have certainly improved private sector business opportunities for Africans, and — at some short-term cost to national economies — have paved the way for broader and faster African business expansion. Beyond this, it is difficult to generalise. Clearly, the scope of any discriminatory measures must be tailored to local capabilities, and, however carefully they are planned, and administered, it is inevitable that some disruption will result. It is the task of governments to keep this disruption to a minimum — partly by assisting suitable Africans to buy businesses which have to be sold and also, more important, by providing appropriate support services to newly-established business-men while they are gaining experience. In this context, at least where Africanisation of commerce is concerned, a useful role might be played by national trading corporations.

National Trading Corporations

All the four countries have national trading corporations of some sort. Each of these was established with the overall objective of promoting African trade; but whereas the corporations in Kenya, Malawi, and Swaziland were all explicitly intended to promote the development of African business in the private sector, Ghana's corporation was established in order to enable the state to challenge foreign domination more directly.

The Ghana National Trading Corporation (GNTC), the oldest of the four corporations, was set up in 1961 in order 'to bring into existence a nation-wide trading organisation owned by the state or the people of Ghana to counteract the country's extreme dependence on foreign firms'. GNTC is larger, and more diverse in its activities, than the corporations in the other three countries. Although its main trading section has more than 7,500 tied credit customers, who earn their living by selling goods for the Corporation on a commission basis, it has not been charged with any responsibility for fostering private sector African business. It has not been concerned with the recent government programmes of assistance, and it welcomed the Ghanaian Business (Promotion) Act on the grounds that it gave wider scope for the representation of overseas suppliers. The Corporation is planning to expand its industrial as well as its trading interests; and with continued government patronage it can be expected to remain profitable. By virtue of administrative discrimination, it already has a number of important monopolies (over the distribution of certain pharmaceuticals, for example), and is obviously in a privileged position with regard to the issue of import licences. In due course, therefore, GNTC's very existence may place a significant brake on the growth of opportunities for Ghanaian private enterprise.

Of the national trading corporations in Kenya, Malawi, and Swaziland, Kenya's is the largest in terms of physical turnover, but Malawi's is of comparable size relative to the national economy and, being considerably more diversified, employs the most staff. Swaziland's, in both absolute and relative terms, is much the smallest. Some of their main characteristics are analysed and compared in Table 2: detailed statistics are for mid-1972.

The Kenya National Trading Corporation (KNTC) has been operating considerably longer than either of the other two (though it should be remembered that Malawi also experimented with a national trading corporation, in partnership with Bookers (Malawi), between 1968 and 1970). On the other hand, although KNTC is the largest in terms of total turnover, IECM already had, by 1972, a wider range of functions and responsibilities, and a larger staff. Since a part of KNTC's turnover merely consists of paper transactions, IECM is also the largest of the corporations in relation to their national economies.

All three corporations are primarily concerned with promoting African trade. All have established networks of wholesale depots, and two of them have monopolies, at some stage in the distribution chain,

Table 2	National Trading Corporations		
	Kenya (KNTC)	Malawi (IECM)	Swaziland (AD)
Established	1965	1971[1]	1971
Size			
Turnover (approx.)	K£18m	K 10m	R 200,000
GNP (approx.)	K£600m	K 320	R 55m
Turnover as % of GNP (approx.)	3	3	less than ½
Staff	265	575	21
Functions			
Monopolies	Yes	Yes	No
Wholesaling (no. of depots)	Yes (26)	Yes (30)	Yes (5)
Credit facilities	No	Yes	No
Associated advisory services	Barely	Planned	Yes
Retailing	No	Yes	No
(Rate of exchange = £1, May 1972	K£0.93	K 2	R 1.94)

[1] IECM's predecessor, the National Trading Corporation, was established in 1968.

for handling certain goods. (Swaziland's Amadoda Distributors (AD) is still too small to be entrusted with monopolies; but it appeared in 1972 that it might soon merge with the country's only other general wholesaler, in which the government – as a consequence of the National Industrial Development Corporation's participation in Kirsh Holdings – had recently taken a 50 percent share, and which, even while it was still wholly privately-owned, had an effective monopoly over the initial distribution of a number of key commodities.) Only IECM offers credit (in strictly limited amounts), KNTC having withdrawn credit facilities, after sustaining undisclosed losses, some years ago, and only AD (through Swaziland's Ministry of Commerce and Co-operatives) is associated with any significant advisory service for African traders.

The most important aspects of comparison, however, are the degree to which the different corporations are committed to foster specifically private-sector Africanisation of trade (where necessary, by abdicating their own operations) and the extent to which they engage in other activities which are less immediately relevant to their prime objective. In 1972 AD's sole task (apart from a contract to supply the Swaziland government with groceries and cleaning materials) was to provide an improved distribution service for African retailers; but KNTC and IECM were both rather more complex institutions.

KNTC was originally given responsibility for a number of trading activities, e.g. in sugar, which were previously carried on by the government; but its operations were intended to be essentially temporary, in that its success would be judged according to the extent to which individual African traders would in due course be able to take them over. Since its establishment, however, it has acquired an institutional momentum which will not easily be stopped, let alone reversed. By 1972, with regard to many commodities, KNTC merely functioned as a regulating body, parcelling out business among its appointed distributors; but the Ndegwa Commission of Inquiry into the Public Service recommended in 1971 that the Corporation should be subjected to a detailed examination aimed at turning it into 'a business organisation in the true sense of the phrase'. KNTC's management, although it has difficulty in recruiting suitable staff, would certainly welcome this, but the government has not yet made any specific response to the Ndegwa recommendation. Nevertheless, it seems clear that, unless it is subjected to a tighter government rein (through its parent company, the Industrial and Commercial Development Corporation), KNTC will become a permanent institution, more closely resembling the national trading corporation in Ghana. KNTC could very easily reach a stage where it actually impeded the further development of private African traders.

IECM, despite the broad scope of its activities, is pursuing an admirably simple strategy. Broadly, this is to break even on its general trading activities and to rely on profits from its Agency, Motors, and Technical Divisions to finance expansion. All its operations are to be transferred, in due course, to private-sector Africans, and the Company's continued involvement in any particular field is to be regularly reviewed. In mid-1972, however, it was too early to judge whether these objectives and principles would be maintained. IECM had not yet introduced a comprehensive training programme, and in this, as in other respects, its success would depend crucially on the quality of its managerial and technical staff. IECM relies fairly heavily on expatriates, and is fortunate in having a particularly able managing director; but, particularly if its key personnel were prematurely replaced by Malawians with insufficient experience, IECM could all too easily become a cumbersome and self-centred bureaucracy.

Conclusion

Discriminatory licensing policies and national trading corporations may both be used, more or less overtly, in order to exclude foreigners from selected business sectors. Moreover, each method can not only be given a universal effect – on the one hand by complete reservation, to local citizens, of certain geographical areas or types of activity, and on the other by monopoly powers which prevent non-citizens from dealing in certain goods – but may also be applied more arbitrarily through the *ad hoc* withdrawal of individual licences or, in the case of a national trading corporation, through day-to-day administrative decisions concerning, for example, the distribution of commodities which happen to be in short supply.

Especially in Kenya and Malawi, it would have taken much longer for African businessmen to become established (and to begin to accumulate the experience which will enable some of them in due course to expand), if the governments concerned had not taken positive steps to loosen the alien grip on the small business sector. So long as evasion can be kept in reasonable check, the surest way to change the business environment in favour of local citizens is to withdraw alien licences; but a delicensing policy may usefully be backed by administrative discrimination applied through a national trading corporation.

A trading corporation may have a particularly important role where – as was the case, at least when discriminatory licensing was first introduced, in both Kenya and Malawi – Africans are not yet capable of taking over large-scale wholesale businesses: by engaging in wholesaling, a government can ensure that African retailers obtain regular supplies at reasonable prices. (In theory the same result can be achieved through price controls; but, particularly if goods are scarce, it is difficult to make such controls effective. Provided that a national trading corporation can be efficiently run it may be more realistic, as well as politically preferable, to by-pass alien wholesalers altogether.) There are additional advantages, political and practical, if the national wholesaler can provide African retailers with credit; but Kenya's experience showed this to be commercially risky, at least unless supported by a broader extension or advisory service. Where the retailers concerned have insufficient experience, unsupervised credit may actually be harmful if it permits them to enter into obligations which they subsequently fail to meet. In mid-1972 it appeared that Malawi's Import and Export Company, then with about 250 credit customers, might already be expanding its credit facilities too fast.

On the other hand, a comprehensive extension service would also be expensive. The most obvious characteristic of bare discriminatory policies, especially of discriminatory licensing, is that, in terms of direct cost to government, they are very cheaply administered. National trading corporations, even if they cover their financial costs, may be more expensive in so far as they absorb scarce manpower; while the institution of an extension service would increase costs substantially. The IECM, for example, would need at least thirty trained extension officers in order to provide a national coverage comparable to that provided in mid-1972 in Swaziland by a single Swazi trade officer assisted by four Peace Corps volunteers. Since the Malawi government would be unlikely to grant IECM a corresponding subsidy, the principal cost of such an extension service would need to be met externally; and with the shortage of appropriate Malawian personnel, it would initially rely on technical assistance both for operational staff and for the training of local replacements. In Kenya, more than 100 extension officers would probably be needed; again, this would require substantial external support and it should be added that in this case it would be preferable, if only in the interests of achieving better coordination among all African business promotion programmes, for the extension staff to be attached to ICDC. They could then also be deployed in giving managerial and financial advice to other categories of business-men operating in the areas they served. Alternatively, in either country, extension officers might be directly employed by the ministry responsible for trade and industry.

The discriminatory policies described in this chapter have so far mainly concentrated on promoting African commerce. In Ghana, however, a few small manufacturing activities have been reserved for citizens, and there appears to be no reason why the sectoral scope of discrimination should not be progressively extended in other countries; for licensing regulations can clearly be applied easily enough to any category of business enterprise. Against this, it should be noted that the trade licensing approach, in so far as it implies the direct transfer of existing alien businesses, presupposes that such businesses are also appropriate both to the personal capacities of their new owners and, more broadly, to the resource endowments of the country concerned. It becomes more important to question these assumptions, as the businesses transferred become more sophisticated; and although African entrepreneurs, including those who start their own businesses from scratch, tend to take alien institutions and methods as a model, it is especially desirable with regard to African-owned industries to enquire whether their size, their technology, and their capital intensity, are wholly suited to local conditions. Other things being equal, it is generally in the African national interest that industries employ as much labour and as little capital as possible; and it may also be necessary to limit the managerial burden which is placed on a single African entrepreneur. In a particular instance, this might imply that, on being 'localised', an individual alien industry would most usefully be broken up into a number of geographically scattered units. There might also be *prima facie* advantages in continuing to link the different units through some form of co-operative organisation; but in none of the four countries does the past record of non-agricultural co-operatives suggest that such an approach would be successful. The technical and organisational aspects of African industry both require further study. Important research is already being done on a rather limited scale by ITDG; this could usefully be expanded, while more attention needs to be paid (within African countries themselves) to the study of institutional structures and business methods.

Finally, with regard to national trading corporations, it should be remarked that these, too, can usefully discriminate in favour of indigenous industry as well as indigenous trade: in particular, they can assist local industries both in the procurement and supply of raw materials and in the marketing and distribution of their products. At the same time, it must be strongly emphasised that this is not an area where experiment should be based on technical feasibility alone. Both the Ghana and the Kenya Corporations might assist existing African manufacturers; but in Malawi, although IECM is enthusiastic to broaden its activities to include industrial promotion, this could be very expensive if the local industries required substantial protection against competing imports, or if their very operation called for large and protracted inputs of technical assistance.

Notes

1. *Economic Report 1972*, Zomba, p. 51.

Chapter 4 Government Loans Schemes

All four countries have operated business loans schemes exclusively or partly for African businessmen, and only Malawi was not operating at least one such scheme in 1972. The main features of these schemes, which are also discussed in their national contexts in Chapters 6—9, are summarised in Table 3 (the two schemes, in Kenya and Swaziland respectively, which are directly linked to the operation of industrial estates, are also considered separately in Chapter 5).

Most of the schemes have offered longer-term loans than would normally be available from commercial banks, usually at comparatively favourable rates of interest. Some form of security has always been required, usually in the form of title deeds or third-party guarantees: relevant security requirements have not been entered in Table 3, however, since these tend to be flexible. Small traders, for example, who often do not possess title deeds, have sometimes been able merely to pledge a charge on their stocks.

With the exception of those run by Ghana's National Investment Bank (NIB) and the Swaziland Credit and Savings Bank (SCSB), all the schemes were designed specifically for African businessmen. In part, at least, they have all been intended to make it easier for African businessmen to acquire capital. Many of the schemes were first introduced before the governments concerned took direct discriminatory action against existing alien business communities: particularly in Kenya, it was felt (initially by the colonial administration) that the provision of African loans might be sufficient in itself to generate African business development, and the failure of early African loans schemes to make a perceptible impact encouraged governments to adopt more definite discriminatory measures, such as were described in the last chapter. On the other hand, since large numbers of alien businessmen had their licences withdrawn, much of the money disbursed through both the Kenyan and the Ghanaian loan schemes has financed business purchase rather than new real investment.

It should be emphasised at the outset that all the schemes have had a strong political motivation; and, especially where a scheme has been administered by the government itself, rather than by a public sector banking institution, the amount lent has generally reflected an arbitrary decision as to what the government could afford rather than any concerted effort to relate the supply of loans to the assessed demand. Of the two Ghanaian schemes, the 1970/71 scheme operated for barely a year, while the NIB extended relatively small amounts of its loan money to the African private sector. Since the Swaziland scheme is also not reserved for Africans, Kenya (at just over 0.3 percent stands out as the country which is currently disbursing the greatest volume of African business loans relative to GNP. With the exception of the ICDC schemes, the total amounts lent to African businessmen have generally been fairly small. This applies particularly to the schemes which have principally catered for retail traders, but even these have apparently been widely enough spread to be of some political importance. Irrespective of a government's desire to foster indigenous private enterprise, an African loans scheme is also an important political symbol and a useful instrument for distributing political favours.

Any government, given the potential patronage which a loans scheme can provide, will prefer to see loans extended to its own supporters. At one extreme, loans may be made to politicians themselves: about 10 percent of the total amount lent under Ghana's 1970/71 small business loans scheme was to members of parliament. The Malawian scheme, on the other hand, seems to have been used (to a greater extent, in terms of the proportion of the total amount lent) as an instrument for compensating deserving members of the Malawi Congress Party who were not rewarded with public office after independence. Political influence can, of course, merely be a screening device; and in economic terms this may not matter much, provided that politically eligible loan applicants also have to satisfy a critical appraisal of their business prospects. In the case of Malawi, however, and also in the case of the smaller schemes operated by Ghana and Kenya, the appraisal procedure was not sufficient to prevent substantial overall rates of default. It must therefore be asked whether the repayment records experienced by these schemes could have been significantly improved, even if political bias had been eliminated.

This is a difficult area for research: first, because lending agencies are reluctant to discuss the degree to which they are subject to political influence and, second, because they usually do not supply information on bad debts. But it is significant that repayments records generally appear to have been better for loans extended through semi-autonomous banks (NIB, ICDC, and SCSB), than for the smaller schemes administered by civil servants. In part, this is attributable to the banks' professional competence, and especially to their more

34

Table 3   Business Loan Schemes

Country	Ghana (1)	Ghana (2)	Kenya (1)
Operated by	Government	NIB	Government
Dates	1970-71	Since 1963	Since mid-1950s
Sectoral scope	Mainly transport & trade	Mainly industry & agriculture	Mainly trade
Limited to Africans	Yes	No	Yes
Approx. annual disbursements (year)	₵6½m (1970/71)	₵11.4m (approved) (1971)	K£125,000 (late 1960s)
% of GNP (approx.)	0.3%	0.5%	0.02%
Limits on size of individual loans	No formal limits	₵10,000+	Up to K£500
Interest rate (most recent)	8%	9%	6½%
Repayment period	1-5 years	3-25 years	Up to 5 years
Appraisal	Regional (up to ₵500); Central (over ₵500)	Bank staff/ Board	District Committees
Follow-up	None	Monthly, by Bank's Post-Finance Dept.	Minimal
Repayments record (approx. default rate)	? Bad (? c. 30%)	? Moderate (not available)	? Bad (? 20-25%)
Rate of exchange (= £1, May 1972)	₵3.31	₵3.31	K£0.93

Key: ICDC   Industrial and Commercial Development Corporation
        NIB   National Investment Bank
        SCSB   Swaziland Credit and Savings Bank.

Kenya (2)			Malawi	Swaziland
ICDC			Government	SCSB
Since late 1950s	Since 1964	Since 1967	Mainly 1958-67	Since 1969
Industry	Commerce	Property	Mainly trade	Mainly trade; some transport
Yes	Yes	Yes	Yes	No
K£320,000 (1970/71)	K£975,000 (1970/71)	K£720,000 (1970/71)	Not available	R195,000 (approved) (1971/72)
0.05%	0.16%	0.12%	Not available	0.3%
K£500+; usually less than K£50,000	K£500-12,500	K£500-20,000	Usually not more than K1,000	R50+
8½%	8½%	9%	5%	9%
5-10 years	3 years	10 years	3-5 years	Up to 5 years
Bank staff/Board	Bank staff/Board	Bank staff/Board	Central Board	Bank staff/Board
Inadequate	Inadequate	Hardly necessary	None	Inadequate
Moderate (14%)	Moderate (8%)	Good (1%)	Bad (? c. 30%)	? Good (not available)
K£0.93	K£0.93	K£0.93	K 2	R 1.94

effective procedures for examining loan applications, but it also reflects that (usually) they are better insulated from political interference. On the other hand, it is clear that, even among proper banking institutions, ICDC, the only one to publish relevant information, has tolerated bad debts on a scale which would not be acceptable to an ordinary commercial bank; and it has done this despite an investment climate considerably better than that in the other countries.

Unfortunately, since governments have often looked at African business loans almost exclusively in political or social terms, there appears to have been little attempt to evaluate the overall economic contribution of any particular scheme. Moreover, very little independent research has been done in this field, in any English-speaking African country, except by S.P. Schatz in Nigeria; a detailed evaluation of any scheme by the present author would have required much freer access to government files and records. Suggestions for improvement must necessarily, therefore, be rather conjectural.

Apart from the question of political bias, there are two obvious ways in which most schemes could improve their performance, as measured by their repayments records. First – and this particularly applies to the schemes directly administered by governments – a higher proportion of the worst risks could be eliminated by a more exhaustive appraisal procedure; but this could only be achieved at considerable cost in terms of money, manpower, and time (which itself might be counter-productive in that delay might significantly prejudice some projects' chances of success). Second, all the schemes analysed in Table 3 have suffered (in the opinion of people concerned with their administration) from inadequate follow-up. Disbursement procedures have usually required the submission of invoices or receipts relating to the goods purchased with money borrowed, but effective follow-up, whatever the purpose of the loan, needs to be much more comprehensive. Even NIB and ICDC have limited their post-finance operations mainly to accounting procedures and have thus ignored the managerial and technical inadequacies which could only be countered by a much broader advisory service.*

More ambitious follow-up would also, of course, make loans schemes correspondingly more expensive, and, with the probable shortage of suitably qualified local personnel, it might be more realistic to accept

---

*   There is the prospect of substantial improvement in this respect in Kenya, if the recent government working party's recommendations are implemented. See Chapter 7.

fairly high rates of default as an operating cost. On the other hand, it should not be inferred from this that conventional loans programmes ought, from any economic standpoint, to be continued at all. Certainly, the proper administration of any loans scheme is likely to be extremely expensive: even existing schemes, although their full operating costs are not usually known, required substantial subsidies. It is significant that both ICDC and SCSB (and probably, also, NIB) have only been able to meet the cost of administering their African loans because they have had access to relatively cheap money and because their overheads have partly been borne by larger-scale business with other clients; and Schatz found even in Nigeria (generally considered to be the most advanced African country with regard to the state of its indigenous private entrepreneurship) that, disregarding bad debt losses attributable to political manipulation of exceptional administrative ineptness, the average aggregate cost to government of each loan made by the Regional Loans Boards in the mid-1960s to a subsequently 'successful' project value of the loan.[1]

Without going into the details of how Schatz arrives at this estimate, one may use his findings to support the argument that special loans schemes represent a fundamentally mistaken approach to African business promotion. It appeared to Schatz that in Nigeria the chief obstacle to private economic development was a shortage of commercially viable projects rather than a shortage of capital. African loans schemes, as presently conceived, totally overlook the real needs of African businessmen. The first priority of any business assistance programme is to design and staff a full range of advisory services; and finance should play no more than a supporting role, in specific instances where considered appraisal of the borrower's business prospects (and history) suggests that it is merited.

Where financial assistance *is* provided, there are strong grounds for charging an interest rate which reflects, at least more nearly than is usually the case at present, the opportunity cost of capital. Outside the commercial banking system, private sector money-lenders often charge rates far in excess of 20 percent p.a. On short- and medium-term borrowing, especially for commerce, it would be quite reasonable for official agencies to charge up to, say, 15 percent. This would discourage political interference, by making financial assistance less attractive as a political instrument, and would reduce the element of subsidy currently given to select groups of African businessmen 'lucky' enough to obtain government loans. For longer term industrial loans it might not be practicable, for realistic cash flow projections, to raise rates so far; but for these loans higher rates would at least serve to favour more labour-intensive investment, which might, in turn, alter the cash flow position in such a way as to make a higher interest rate more feasible.

At the same time, it should be emphasised that, however high the interest rate, it could not permit a small business advisory service, directly operating its own loans scheme, to be financially self-supporting. The higher the rate, the harder it would be for the advisory service to find businesses capable of servicing a loan; and although higher rates could to some extent offset the cost of loan supervision, they would be partly self-defeating in so far as they directly contributed to more defaults. There are very few African countries – of which Ghana is one – in which many African businessmen can conceivably qualify, on rational criteria, for individual loans large enough for all the cost of the associated appraisal and follow-up procedure to be financed out of interest payments (particularly if the lending institution is itself paying anything approaching the international market rate on its capital). More important, even in these countries, governments must accept that they cannot hope to give smaller businessmen the help they require, without incurring budgetary expenditure which will not be directly recoverable.

Where a government does undertake a small business development programme, it should constantly seek to help individual businessmen, once they have reached a certain level of sophistication and proven competence, to obtain finance from the existing commercial banking system. Special lending schemes, quite apart from their potential for abuse, do not break down the characteristic barriers between African businessmen and the broader business communities of which they must hope to become an integral part. Therefore, although it may be necessary to make special government provision for relatively long-term loans (mainly for industry), government schemes to provide short-term capital should be regarded as a temporary expedient at best. It is greatly preferable for short-term finance to be obtained from commercial banks, if necessary with the help of a government-sponsored guarantee scheme.

Notes

1. S.P. Schatz, *Economics, Politics and Administration in Government Lending,* Oxford University Press, London, 1970, Chapter 7.

Chapter 5 Industrial Estates

In 1972 Kenya and Swaziland (but not Ghana or Malawi) were both promoting private-sector African industry by installing and assisting selected entrepreneurs on specially reserved estates. (Kenya Industrial Estates (KIE) and Swaziland's Small Enterprises Development Company (SEDCO) are considered separately, in their national context (in Chapter 7 and Chapter 9). Although their objectives and operations were in some respects markedly different, there are enough similarities for the two programmes to be directly compared.

The prime motivation behind each programme was again socio-political rather than purely economic. In most African countries, particularly outside West Africa, medium- to large-scale industry (and also, even, virtually everything that in most advanced countries would be described as 'small-scale' industry) has mainly been developed, owned, and controlled by non-Africans. As in commerce, this alien domination has been tacitly, if not openly, resented. Although, in some countries, important expatriate industries have been wholly or partially nationalised, it is not surprising — in view of the greater cost of assisting African industrialists and the greater demands which industry places on the managerial and technical skills of entrepreneurs — that efforts to develop the local private sector have initially concentrated on promoting African trade. Where a government does undertake a programme of assistance to African industry, however, there are obvious advantages in constructing one or more special industrial estates. Quite apart from the resulting ease of administration, and the opportunity for provision of common services, potential African industrialists are assumed to require improved accommodation and equipment as well as technical and managerial assistance. Such estates are also politically attractive since, compared to less intensive schemes, which would concentrate on assisting and improving established industries without moving them to a new location, they provide more tangible symbols of modern African industrial development.

Industrial estates also appeal to aid donors: both KIE and SEDCO have been heavily dependent, since their inception, on foreign capital and technical assistance. The construction of KIE's first estate, at Nairobi, which has taken place in two phases, was largely financed by

loans from the West German Kreditanstalt für Wiederaufbau (KfW), and
technical support has been received from both Germany and India. The
KfW is also lending substantial support for KIE's second estate, at
Nakuru, and in 1972 the Kenya government was seeking external
assistance for the building of further estates at Kisumu, Mombasa, and
Eldoret. Exploratory discussions on financing at least one of these have
been held with the Swedish International Development Agency (SIDA).

SEDCO was established after a report to the Swaziland government
by ILO's regional adviser for small enterprises, who later returned to
Swaziland under UN technical assistance and became manager of a
UNDP/ILO project for small enterprises and handicraft development. In
mid-1972, the Company planned to build a total of about seven small
estates in different parts of Swaziland, each estate specialising in a
particular activity appropriate to its geographical location. Three estates
were already properly established — in Manzini (metalwork), Piggs Peak
(woodwork), and Mbabane (where the range of products is rather wider
than elsewhere and includes clothing, jewellery, pottery, and artificial
flowers). UNDP was supplying a technical assistance team of nine
experts (only five of whom were in post by June 1972), supporting
equipment, and fellowships for Swazi counterparts; and Britain, having
financed about 80 percent of the estates' construction costs, was
providing a substantial part of Swaziland's 'local' contribution to the
UN project. Work had been started on at least one more estate, at
Siteki; and it should also be noted (see Chapter 9) that SEDCO has
been concerned with other aspects of entrepreneurial development,
outside the estates programme. Only the three established estates,
however, will be discussed in the present chapter.

Detailed information about KIE and SEDCO is contained in Table 4.
The inclusion of so many exact figures should not be taken to imply
that all are equally reliable. The estimates of working capital, which in
both cases roughly correspond to the total accounts contributed by the
entrepreneurs themselves, are necessarily very approximate, especially
for SEDCO, as are the SEDCO expenditures on machinery and
equipment and even the figures for the SEDCO estates' respective total
outputs. Taken together, however, the figures do allow broad comparison.

It will be seen that the total capital employed at KIE (in June 1971)
was more than twice as great, both in absolute terms and in relation to
employment, as the average for SEDCO (in March 1972). Part of this
investment — the administration block and the technical service
centre — also serves the factories constructed under the second phase of

the estate's development, and it will be shared by the other proposed estates and (probably) Kenya's Rural Industrial Development Programme. On the other hand the figures in Table 4 do not include the machinery, valued at £26,500, donated by India for the technical service centre. This centre, which provides (at cost) servicing and repair facilities for all the industries on the estate, has been operating far below capacity. Common facility equipment was also to be provided on the SEDCO estates, but in 1972 much of this had not yet been installed: it was to be paid for by UNDP and, again, its cost is not included in Table 4.

The Nairobi estate, despite its smaller significance in relation to GDP, does represent a much more ambitious attempt to create African *industry*. In terms of average area, the individual units are more than three times as large as SEDCO's, and they are engaged in a wider range of relatively sophisticated activities, including the manufacture of various metal, wooden, and textile products, and printing. In the planning of the estate, each project was subjected to a detailed feasibility study by German and Kenyan staff of KIE. These studies concentrated too much on abstract technical aspects of the industries concerned and (partly, perhaps, because 'entrepreneurs' were not selected until after the studies had been completed) paid insufficient attention to prospective management problems, particularly marketing: several industries, especially those intended for import substitution and dependent on government protection (which has not always been successfully enforced), have had considerable difficulty in establishing markets which can absorb the minimum turnover necessary for viability. The feasibility studies were also much too optimistic in assuming that it would generally be sufficient for entrepreneurs to prove that they could themselves contribute working capital equivalent to their requirements for only three months. Many entrepreneurs have had severe cash flow problems; and although by mid-1972 there was the prospect of some relief through a scheme whereby a commercial bank would finance bulk purchases of raw materials by KIE for sale to individual entrepreneurs on a cash retail basis, there remained the problem of too much capital tied up in unsold stocks.

KIE's management (like SEDCO's) does not know exactly how individual businesses are faring. But although by mid-1972 only one had closed down, only about one-third of the businesses were making a reasonable profit and perhaps another third were running at a loss. More than half the businesses were irregular over rent payments; but since arrears were not subject to even a token penalty, this in itself did

42

Table 4

Kenya Industrial
Estates (KIE)
(30 June 1971)

	Nairobi (Phase I)
Commencement of operations	1968
Capital Expenditure	
Buildings etc.	K£194,000
Machinery & equipment	150,000
Working Capital	94,000
Total	K£438,000
Sterling equivalent	£470,000
Number of units	25
Capital cost/unit	K£17,500
Sterling equivalent	£18,800
Government investment/unit	K£13,750
Sterling equivalent	£14,800
Area/unit (sq.ft.)	625-3,750
Rents (per sq.ft./month)	K£0.025
Sterling equivalent	2.7p
Total Turnover (per annum)	K£245,000
% of GDP (approx.)	0.04%
Capital/Turnover ratio	1.8
Value added (per annum)	K£75,000
Employment	370
Capital cost/employee	K£1,200
Sterling equivalent	£1,300
Government investment/employee	K£ 925
Sterling equivalent	£1,000
Rate of exchange (= £1, May 1972)	K£0.93

**Small Enterprises Development Company
(SEDCO), Swaziland
(31 March 1972)**

Mbabane	Manzini	Piggs Peak	Total
1970	1971	1970	
R75,000	R25,000	R22,000	R122,000
60,000	20,000	20,000	100,000
70,000	13,000	12,000	95,000
R205,000	R58,000	R54,000	R317,000
£105,000	£30,000	£28,000	£164,000
24	12	10	46
R8,500	R4,800	R5,400	R6,900
£4,400	£2,500	£2,800	£3,550
R5,600	R3,750	R4,200	R4,800
£2,900	£1,950	£2,150	£2,500
	Mainly 180-500 (a few are larger)		
	R0.04 — 0.05		
	2.1p — 2.6p		
R200,000	R40,000	R20,000	R260,000
0.37%	0.07%	0.05%	0.5%
1.0	1.5	2.7	1.1
	not available		
206	44	25	275
R1,000	R1,300	R2,200	R1,150
£ 515	£ 670	£1,130	£ 590
R 650	R1,000	R1,700	R 810
£ 340	£ 525	£ 865	£ 415

R1.94

not indicate financial difficulty.

The development of the SEDCO estates has followed a rather different pattern. Since the enterprises were less capital-intensive, individual entrepreneurs could commence operations on a very much smaller scale, in some cases even with no paid employees, and they have been able to delay expansion until it was clearly justified. It is significant that, in mid-1972, much the larger part of the total output on the Mbabane estate was contributed by just three enterprises. Each had been greatly expanded in the previous two years; and, between them, they must have accounted for much the greater part of the R70,000 which was the estimated working capital contribution of all the entrepreneurs on the Mbabane estate (see Table 4). SEDCO's entrepreneurs, who also have direct access to South African export and tourist markets, have thus been permitted to adjust the scale of their operations more easily, according to both their capability and their market. (By mid-1972 only one enterprise had failed – merely from trying to expand too rapidly.) There is the additional national advantage, derived from the relative labour-intensity and craft nature of the SEDCO enterprises, that their value added, in relation to turnover, is almost certainly considerably in excess of the average (barely 30 percent) for KIE.

But KIE and SEDCO have several features in common. In addition to offering rented accommodation at sub-market rates, each runs a scheme to help entrepreneurs with purchase of their machinery and equipment. In the case of KIE, selected entrepreneurs are automatically eligible for ICDC loans, at 8½ percent interest and repayable over nine years, for the purchase of all their machinery. SEDCO's entrepreneurs are able to buy equipment up to R10,000 in value on hire purchase: the exact arrangements vary but, typically, the entrepreneur makes an initial 10 percent deposit, and the remaining 90 percent is paid over two to three years (never more than five years) with interest calculated throughout at 7 percent of the full capital cost. SEDCO's terms – despite the fact that they include insurance of the equipment concerned – are thus considerably more onerous; but since capital requirements are usually fairly small, most entrepreneurs have been able to meet them. The SEDCO terms may also constitute an incentive to employ relatively labour-intensive techniques.

The most obvious common characteristic of the two schemes (apart, perhaps, from their political motivation) is their apparent expensiveness. Even allowing for the prospective sharing of some of KIE's overheads by the Nairobi estate's phase II, and by the other estates which are to be established elsewhere in the country, and for the fact that in both Kenya and Swaziland (particularly at Piggs Peak) many units have been operating below their installed capacity, small industrial estates clearly involve an intensive input of capital and technical assistance.

The estimates of average capital cost per employee (see Table 4) would in any case be considerably larger if full allowance were made for net operating costs. KIE had a net accumulated 'loss', at 30 June 1971, of K£109,000, and, even if only half of this is capitalised and ascribed to Nairobi's phase I, the figures for government investment go up by more than 15 percent. SEDCO, although its book losses up to 1972 had been negligible, has relied on administrative support from SEPO (see Chapter 10), whose costs are included in Swaziland's ordinary recurrent budget and whose total locally-financed expenditure for 1972–73, including a general grant to the UN project amounting to R17,500, was estimated at nearly R42,000.

The real cost of external technical assistance should also be taken into account. Although in Kenya this may have a low opportunity cost, in the sense that it might not have been possible to transfer the German and Indian assistance concerned to other uses, the same cannot be said for UN technical assistance to SEDCO, which must be debited to Swaziland's UNDP country programme. (It should be noted that although the present UN project is due to end in March 1975, and a small number of individual enterprises may by then be capable of carrying on unaided, it is very unlikely that the local counterparts of the UN experts will be in a position to maintain the estates programme, after that date, without continued technical assistance.) Finally, an evaluation of KIE should also allow for the economic cost (particularly if, as is possible, this will be a lasting commitment) of protecting relatively inefficient domestic industries against cheaper imports from abroad.

In view of the difficulty in determining at this stage, and on the basis of the limited information available, exactly what costs are attributable to Nairobi's phase I and to SEDCO's first three estates, rather than to other aspects of the KIE and Swaziland programmes, any attempt to quantify all these factors would probably be misleading. On the basis of the figures in Table 4, however, it is possible, using the ratios of capital expenditure to employment, to estimate the cost, in both Kenya and Swaziland, of creating employment opportunities for the whole of the target increases to wage-employment. In Kenya, it would cost a total of K£84m per annum, including government investment of K£65m, to meet the current Development Plan target of 70,000 new wage-paid jobs every year; this compares with actual 1971 total domestic fixed capital formation estimated at K£131m, of which £30m was by the government. Swaziland, in order to absorb an annual net increase to the labour force estimated at about 4,500, would require total investment of R5.2m, including R3.6m by the government, compared to actual investment of R11.2m in 1967–68 (the last year for which national accounts are available) and estimated 1971–72 total government investment of R3.55m.

The Swaziland government's budgeted capital expenditure for 1972–73 was R10.3m (representing an increase of nearly 200 percent); this confirms that Swaziland's industrial estates programme is considerably cheaper than Kenya's in terms of its demand on national resources. This does not, of course, imply that Swaziland's programme is necessarily better; though it should also be remembered that the SEDCO programme is essentially export-oriented, whereas the success of KIE partly depends on effective protection from foreign competition. In the absence of fuller information, both about the place of each programme in its respective national economy and about the prosperity or otherwise of individual enterprises on the different estates, it is not possible to assess, more precisely, the relative benefits of the two programmes.

It can be said, in favour of KIE, that its industries are more closely geared to the country's industrial needs, that they can be expanded in step with the rest of the economy, and that Kenyan industrialists perhaps therefore have better prospects of proper integration within the expatriate-dominated industrial sector. Furthermore, the nature of Kenya's tourist market would probably not have favoured an approach which, like Swaziland's, was heavily biased towards handicrafts. Nevertheless, the Kenya government might have been better advised to conceive KIE on a more modest scale. It would even have been preferable, at the country's present stage of development, to concentrate first on the rural industrial development programme. (The plans for Kenya's rural industrial development centres are outlined in Chapter 7, where it is also urged that, instead of being exclusively concerned with industry, these should be general business promotion centres, concerned with the propagation and co-ordination of all types of assistance.)

The future of industrial estates programmes depends considerably on the attitudes of external aid agencies. African governments will certainly continue to want to establish such estates; but at the same time, partly because of the need for associated technical assistance, it is unlikely that they will finance them with their own capital. Moreover, although there is certainly scope, throughout Africa, for more small-scale industries, it is by no means proved that their characteristic benefits — for example, their labour intensity and adaptability, their demonstration effects, and the fact that they facilitate a wider participation in the modern economy — are maximised by concentrating small industrial development in special estates. Aid donors who are genuinely concerned with development, rather than with political relations and show-piece projects, should therefore examine the context of any industrial estate proposal very carefully in order to see whether, even within the African business sector, the same effort might not more usefully be dispersed among a larger number of entrepreneurs, spread over a wider geographical area. We shall return to this question in the concluding chapter.

Part II

Chapter 6 Ghana

Economic and Political Background

Ghana has long been the richest of the four countries included in this study — but its economic growth-rate, in terms of real income per head, was virtually nil throughout the 1960s. In 1969, gross national product amounted to 2,285 million Cedis (equivalent at that time to £930m), corresponding to a per caput income of about £110. By 1972, following a relaxation of controls by the Busia government which first stimulated the economy and then precipitated a balance of payments crisis, a massive devaluation, and the country's second military coup, the Ghanaian economy seemed to be in a worse state than at any time since independence (1957). The new government, led by Colonel Acheampong, undertook to pursue a vigorous policy, based on the principle of 'self-reliance', aimed at increasing domestic production (particularly of food) and reducing the budgetary deficit; but such a policy requires considerable political fortitude and administrative capacity.

The ruling National Redemption Council (NRC) is Ghana's fourth government since 1957, and the substantial political changes of the past fifteen years have been accompanied by a marked swing back and forth in the government attitude towards private Ghanaian businessmen. In the first few years following independence, the Nkrumah government appeared to give them some encouragement; but despite a modest distribution of political spoils (through preferential treatment and loans programmes), the accent was on statements of policy rather than practical schemes of assistance. As from about 1961, the government — perhaps disillusioned by the country's slow progress towards economic independence — adopted an overtly socialist policy; and notwithstanding Peter Garlick's finding, in 1966, that the great majority of the larger African businessmen in Accra whom he had interviewed six to seven years previously were still in business,[1] the closing years of the Nkrumah regime were not easy ones for private sector development. Nkrumah stated his own position quite clearly in March 1964: 'We would be hampering our advance to socialism if we were to encourage the growth of Ghanaian private capitalism in our midst.'

51

Following the 1966 coup, the military National Liberation Council (NLC) took a more favourable attitude towards the private sector; and after the return to civilian rule in 1969, Dr. Busia's government introduced measures for the positive promotion and encouragement of Ghanaian business. These were specifically directed towards assisting Ghanaian citizens, and they discriminated against non-Ghanaians; but the government repeatedly emphasised that it was merely intended to exclude non-Ghanaians from certain areas of the private sector. Otherwise, the government publicly adopted a favourable attitude towards all private entrepreneurship. The economic expansion of 1969–71 also provided a market incentive for the private sector, but the continuing structural weakness of Ghana's economy was soon reflected in a critical deterioration in the balance of external payments. In December 1971 the government took panic steps to improve the situation; a month later, in January 1972, it was deposed.

The NRC announced a policy that 'the reconstituted Ghanaian Enterprises Advisory Committee should take on the additional responsibility of reviewing immediately the provisions of the Ghanaian Business (Promotion) Act to ensure rapid economic growth as well as an increase of Ghanaian participation in the economic activities of the country'. Nevertheless, given Ghana's present economic predicament, the immediate prospects for all businessmen are very poor. In mid-1972, the NRC was intending to cut 1972 imports to little more than half their 1971 level (in terms of Cedis). Imports of non-essential consumer goods were being drastically reduced; and since most importing is in the hands of non-Ghanaians (and GNTC), who would now need to keep a higher proportion of their quota for their own purposes, Ghanaian businesses were in an especially weak position. Many of the smallest traders had already sold off their stock and gone out of business, hoping to resume in better times, but larger businessmen cannot adjust the scale of their operations so easily. It was stated that priority was being given, in the issue of import licences, to agriculture and industry; but several industries depending on imported raw materials were known to have received licences, supposedly for the whole of 1972, sufficient to cover only three to four months' needs. Particularly if the government enforced its instruction that workers were only to be dismissed in cases of genuine misconduct, many Ghanaian businessmen appeared to face substantial losses or even liquidation. The government did subsequently issue increased import licences for raw materials; but as a result of continued stringency on imports of consumer goods, by the end of the year many more traders had been driven out of business.

Without such drastic measures, there is probably no prospect of remedying the chronic structural weakness of Ghana's economy. With external credit virtually unobtainable, Ghana has no option but to become more self-sufficient, particularly in food, and to tailor its demand for luxury imports to what it can afford. Any process of successful readjustment will inevitably be very painful while it lasts. But fundamental changes are a prerequisite to any sustainable expansion of Ghana's economy, and without the latter, there can be no prospect of a better climate for investment (by Ghanaians or by non-Ghanaians) in the private sector.

The Present State of African Entrepreneurship

With regard to local entrepreneurship, Ghana (in common with other West African countries, notably Nigeria) has a much longer commercial tradition than the other countries included in this study. Market women have a long-established role in small retail trade, and some of them have built up substantial business interests and are an important source of finance for other businesses. The boom conditions of the 1940s and early 1950s enabled many Ghanaians to accumulate savings; and despite the relative stagnation of the last fifteen years, there are several Ghanaian entrepreneurs (mainly men) whose businesses are larger and more sophisticated than those of their counterparts in East and Southern Africa. But each of these characteristically maintains strict personal control over his business operations. There is the minimum of delegation, even where the entrepreneur has branched out into a conglomerate of different, sometimes quite unrelated, businesses, and because of widespread mutual distrust there are few successful partnerships.

There are no official statistics concerning the size of the African business sector. Ghanaians are well-established in trade and in road transport; and although large-scale trade — particularly import-export business — is largely in the hands of expatriate companies and the state-owned Ghana National Trading Corporation (GNTC), Ghanaian traders — particularly since the implementation of the 1970 Ghanaian Business (Promotion) Act (GBPA) — are becoming increasingly important at intermediate levels of the distribution chain. This is largely at the expense of Lebanese and Indians, against whom the GBPA was principally directed. At least in theory, by 1972 Ghanaians owned and operated virtually all trading businesses with an annual turnover of less than ₵500,000 (about £150,000); but most larger businesses, including the major department stores and supermarkets in urban areas, continued to be owned by Europeans, Asians, Lebanese, or GNTC.

So far as directly productive activities are concerned, there is a mass of relatively small Ghanaian craftsmen, but it is impossible to be specific about their number or their contribution to GNP. A 1963 sample survey of small manufacturing establishments employing nine or less people has not been repeated; in any case this did not distinguish between Ghanaian and non-Ghanaian ownership. More recent statistics, published in August 1970 and covering establishments with thirty or more employees in 1966–68, do distinguish Ghanaian from non-Ghanaian ownership but do not identify the proportion owned by the state. It is clear, however, that in Ghana, Africans have a much greater and more diverse share in the industrial sector, than they do in the other countries in this study. Although the largest industries are still foreign- or state-owned, private Ghanaian industries produce a wide range of consumer goods including processed foods, soft drinks, textiles, clothing, furniture, handbags, suitcases, mattresses, and cosmetics. There is also a relatively large number of Ghanaian contractors. In May 1972, 364 Ghanaian enterprises were registered with the Public Works Department for various classes of government building or road-work contract; and except for civil engineering and the largest building projects, most government work is now contracted to Ghanaians.

The Busia government estimated that about 600 alien businesses would be affected by the GBPA, but it seems to have had little idea of the size of the existing African private sector. It is unlikely that any attempt will be made in the foreseeable future to obtain more detailed information, since the NRC is still grappling with larger and more immediate problems. In a sense, however, the absolute size of the African business sector is in any case irrelevant, since the majority of Ghanaian businessmen still seek to have as few relations with government as possible. The unprecedentedly severe import licence restrictions introduced in 1972 restored the opportunity (which had been partially removed by the relaxation of controls under Busia) for quick profit to anyone able to obtain a licence which he does not want to use himself; and many of the most promising entrepreneurial opportunities still lie in other economically parasitic practices such as smuggling. Even among more conventional businessmen, the majority are, almost certainly, successfully evading tax.

Government Programmes of Assistance

The measures introduced by the Busia government were largely concerned with localising the existing non-African private sector and (in order to facilitate this) with making it easier for Ghanaian businessmen to obtain short-term loans. They were foreshadowed in 1968 by the NLC's Promotion of Ghanaian Business Enterprises Decree. In 1968 the newly-elected civil government ordered the deportation of all aliens lacking valid residence permits; and in July 1970 the NLC Decree was superseded by the Ghanaian Business (Promotion) Act. The latter was backed by a scheme for the official guarantee of commercial bank credit and by a new Small Business Loan Scheme. A special Office of Business Promotion (OBP) was also established; and, independently of OBP, the ILO-assisted Management Development and Productivity Institute set up a new division, the Ghanaian Business Bureau, specifically to provide advisory, consulting and training services for Ghanaian businessmen.

The Ghanaian Business (Promotion) Act has already been described in Chapter 3. It will suffice, here, to repeat that its main objective was to reserve certain sectors of the economy for Ghanaians and that, in so far as it accelerated the transfer to Ghanaians of businesses which they were for the most part competent to run, it has been reasonably successful. The same cannot be said for the Small Business Loan Scheme (see Chapter 4). Introduced in December 1970, this was the latest of a number of loan schemes designed to meet the needs of Ghanaian businessmen: the three principal schemes instituted before independence (by the Industrial Development Corporation, the Ghana Guarantee Corporation, and the Cocoa Purchasing Company) all experienced heavy defaults, partly, no doubt, as a result of their being used for political purposes, and it appears that the government will be lucky if it recovers as much as 70 percent of the amount lent under the 1970 scheme. A total of about ₵6½m was disbursed in the twelve months of the scheme's operation. But, in terms both of the sums involved and of its broader relevance to the business promotion programmes of other African countries, the credit guarantee scheme is much more important. This, together with the provision of finance by the National Investment Bank, is discussed in the section on financial institutions below.

At least in principle, the establishment of the Office of Business Promotion (OBP) was also a significant step. Set up in 1970, this was intended to serve the Ghanaian Enterprises Advisory Committee (which, as explained elsewhere, appears to have played little part in framing government policy) and also, particularly by assisting Ghanaians with the problems of purchasing alien businesses, to help in the implementation of the Ghanaian Business (Promotion) Act. In its first year, the Office's staff was too small and too inexperienced to take any important role in the purchase negotiations following the Business Promotion Act: these were left to private treaty, and the OBP was mainly concerned with administering loans approved by the government committees responsible for the Small Business Loan Scheme. In mid-1972, the OBP was trying to recover these loans. Its staff had been strengthened, particularly through the appointment (in 1971) of an experienced state enterprise manager as senior executive; and there were nine senior officers at the Accra headquarters, with an additional officer in each Region to serve as secretary to the local loans committee. The new senior executive had ambitious plans for OBP's expansion to provide a wide-ranging extension service, partly through absorption of the Management Development and Productivity Institute's Ghanaian Business Bureau. But it seemed unlikely that these would be accepted by the NRC. OBP's past and continuing association with the loans scheme (now in wide disrepute) seemed to discount any real possibility – even assuming the necessary government resources were available – of its early use as a central co-ordinating agency. Nevertheless, OBP loans, restricted to purposes of manufacture or export, were resumed on a small scale in January 1973.

The various measures introduced by the Busia administration conspicuously lacked any effective means of co-ordination. There was never, for example, any proper definition of the intended relationship between the OBP and the Ghanaian Business Bureau (GBB). The Management Development and Productivity Institute (MDPI) was at first mainly concerned with running management courses designed primarily to meet the needs of large public or expatriate enterprises. But by 1972 the Institute was giving increasing emphasis to consultancy and on-the-job training, both for managers and for self-employed entrepreneurs. Its larger-scale activities are still largely concentrated on public enterprises; but since March 1971 a separate division, the Ghanaian Business Beureau, has been responsible for advising and training Ghanaian entrepreneurs. In 1972 GBB had two branches, in Accra and Kumasi. In addition to running management courses, short conferences, 'workshops' (concerned with matters which need to be considered by people starting new businesses) and 'clinics' (dealing with specific problems of small businessmen within a particular industry), the Bureau offers individual advice to Ghanaian businessmen — both on a general consultancy basis and in relation to specific problems of marketing, accounting, finance, product analysis, production management, record-keeping, and so on.

Unlike the rest of MDPI, GBB is not supported by ILO. Its establishment was based on the recruitment of five Peace Corps volunteers, all with several years' business experience in the United States, who were personally interviewed and selected by MDPI's Ghanaian Director, from a short list of seven compiled by the Peace Corps. The selected volunteers attended a training course in Accra, run by a specially-imported firm of US consultants, before the Bureau opened. By mid-1972, when it had been operating for just over a year, it was possible to make some assessment of the Bureau's work.

GBB's two branches have operated largely independently of one another, and MDPI's Director has allowed them fairly wide autonomy. Since they have also had few relations with other government agencies, their evolution has depended almost entirely on the initiative of the individual volunteers and their Ghanaian counterparts (most of whom, regrettably, were not appointed in time to attend the initial training course). Originally, two volunteers were assigned to Accra and three to Kumasi: by mid-1972, there was only one volunteer in Accra, with three counterparts, but there were still three volunteers, with a total of four counterparts, in Kumasi. Both branches were mainly concentrating on personal consultancy rather than courses, and it was clear that the Kumasi branch had been much more successful in gaining the confidence both of Ghanaian entrepreneurs and of the wider business community. (This was partly a reflection of the Kumasi branch's larger size, and the fact that it was operating in a more compact environment — one which was less dominated by large expatriate and state enterprises — so that it had been easier to build up a local reputation.) Even the Kumasi branch found that some businessmen tended to approach it only as a last resort, when their businesses were already in severe difficulty; but it was undoubtedly playing an important role in assisting its clients with their internal technical and managerial problems and in helping them to establish and strengthen external business relationships (particularly with the commercial banks). In response to client requests, it was offering a consultancy service to Ghanaian farmers as well as to industry and (to a lesser extent) commerce, and it had regular contacts with some sixty to seventy entrepreneurs.

GBB is still in the early stages of its evolution, and no one has yet appraised its work.[2] Meanwhile, although in mid-1972 there was no definite plans for continued Peace Corps support after 1973, it was clear that this would be needed if the programme was to be usefully maintained. It should also be noted that GBB's isolation from other government programmes (and particularly the fact that it was not associated with any loan scheme) had at least protected it from political influence and distortion. On the other hand, GBB would need substantially increased government support, backed by external technical assistance, to make a really significant national impact. The existing scale of GBB's activities, particularly in Accra, had no obvious rationale except as a pilot experiment. Subject to a thorough study and evaluation of its achievements, GBB (particularly if the government is unwilling to develop the Office of Business Promotion) might form the basis of a wider and more ambitious extension service.

Finally, it is interesting in the context of this study that the Peace Corps volunteers possessed a combination of qualifications, experience, and energetic enthusiasm such as is rarely available through other technical assistance programmes. It might be very hard to recruit comparable 'volunteers' (paid enough to support themselves and their families at a comfortable standard of living) in Britain. In any case, British technical assistance channels (including the British Volunteer Programme) are not currently geared to finding or attracting people of this sort.

Financial Institutions

Government loans schemes for Ghanaian businessmen have already been described. This section considers the National Investment Bank (NIB) and the ordinary commercial banks. The NIB, together with one of the three commercial banks, is within the public sector, and since most commercial bank lending to African businessmen is covered by an official credit guarantee scheme, the government has substantial influence over the role of financial institutions generally.

The National Investment Bank, established in 1963, provides equity and loan capital, principally for industry and agriculture. New equity share-holdings, which in the Bank's early years were mainly in state enterprises, are largely concentrated in joint ventures with foreign investors. Ghanaian businessmen have been more affected by NIB's loans programme, which has already been referred to in Chapter 4. At 31 December 1971, outstanding loans (excluding loans approved but not yet utilised) totalled ¢14.7m, of which ¢12.1m was with predominantly private-sector borrowers. The Bank would not disclose what proportion was owned by private-sector Ghanaians. Its lower lending limit, of ¢10,000, has placed it out of reach of many smaller businessmen, and in 1969 it failed to take advantage of an AID proposal to sponsor a special Revolving Fund, whose Articles would have incorporated an incentive to make relatively small loans to Ghanaian businessmen. The Bank was in any case perhaps not suited to administer such a fund. More significant, as an indication of the scale of some Ghanaian entrepreneurs, is the fact that, despite the Bank's stipulation that its borrowers should themselves finance at least 25 percent of the cost of any project, it claimed by 1972 to be making many Ghanaian loans of between ¢50,000 and ¢100,000.

Applications for NIB loans are appraised by the Bank's Development Services Institute (containing sixteen professional officers in mid-1972), which also provides a consultancy service, including the preparation of feasibility studies, not necessarily restricted to existing or prospective clients. In addition, the Bank's Post-Finance Department (containing four accountants in mid-1972) keeps a check on borrowers and helps them improve their record-keeping. This department was to be expanded, and it was planned that its advisory facilities, like those of the Development Services Institute, should be available to non-customers at an economic fee.

In terms of volume of money, and to an even greater extent in terms of numbers of loans, the NIB (although its money is generally lent for longer periods – 3–25 years) is a relatively insignificant source of finance for private Ghanaian businessmen, when compared to the commercial banks. There are three main commercial banks operating in Ghana: Ghana Commercial Bank (the youngest but also the largest, with about 60 percent of total deposits), Standard Bank Ghana, and Barclays Bank of Ghana. (In addition, the Ghana Post Office Savings Bank was due to become semi-commercial in August 1972.) In December 1971, a total of ¢175m was outstanding to these from the private sector; and although relevant figures are not published, it may be estimated that the share of this attributable to Ghanaian business-men was in the order of 10 percent (¢15–20m).

Compared to their counterparts in many other African countries, the commercial banks in Ghana thus have a fairly important stake in African business development. Nevertheless, the banks have encoun-tered the usual problems – inadequate security, bad debts and poor profitability – in trying to increase their lending to Africans. Aware of these difficulties, the government introduced a scheme in December 1969 for the partial guarantee of commercial bank credit. Planned with technical assistance from the Reserve Bank of India and administered by a special Development Finance Division in the Bank of Ghana (Ghana's central bank), the scheme was intended not only to increase the total volume of African lending, but also to encourage the banks to lend more to certain 'priority' sectors such as agriculture, industry, and mining. The scheme is backed by a special fund, set aside by the Bank of Ghana, which must at all times amount to at least 10 percent of the total amount guaranteed.

The government has required all advances to small Ghanaian borrowers, granted, renewed or increased on or after 1 December 1969, to be covered. 'Small borrowers' include proprietary concerns, partnerships or companies which satisfy the following criteria:

(i)   In industry, transport, or servicing industry, individual units must have a total fixed investment in plant and machinery not exceeding ₵50,000.

(ii) In trade, individual units must have total annual sales not exceeding ₵300,000.

(iii) In agriculture, eligible borrowers must normally have not more than 100 acres under cultivation of cash crops (excluding cocoa).

(iv) In livestock and poultry farming, the total capital cost of any project must not exceed ₵50,000.

Initially, bank lending to Ghanaians was eligible for a two-thirds guarantee, subject to a maximum claim of ₵50,000. Subsequently, following the passage of the Ghanaian Business (Promotion) Act, 75 percent cover (with a maximum claim of ₵75,000) was made available to finance the Ghanaian purchase of alien businesses, and since September 1970 a full 100 percent guarantee (with maximum claim of ₵100,000) has been available, on request from the customer and subject to Bank of Ghana approval, with respect to any loan, for manufacturing or agriculture, which a commercial bank has been unwilling to consider on any other basis. In all cases, the lending institution pays, to the Bank of Ghana, a commission of 1 percent per annum of the maximum advance. (With respect to loans which are two-thirds guaranteed, the Bank therefore receives 1½ percent of its liability.) Moreover, the Bank has the power to set the rate of interest charged by the lender. In May 1972 this was 11 percent, which was low by contemporary Ghanaian standards. (Interest-rates on other commercial bank lending ranged up to about 15 percent, while the banks were themselves paying as much as 8 percent on fixed deposits.)

It is hardly surprising, in the light of these provisions, that the scheme has not been much welcomed by the banks. The managements of the public sector lending institutions were probably disappointed when, on the scheme's introduction, the two privately-owned banks did not make more forceful representations for greater freedom in its use, or at least on the interest-rate to be charged. From the government's point of view, the scheme has also been disappointing in that it has not re-directed significant amounts of lending towards the priority sectors. Overall, bank lending to Ghanaians has certainly increased, but only a relatively small part of this increase should be attributed to the scheme. At the end of March 1972, nearly 5,000 loans, with a total value of ₵19.1m, were guaranteed, and 83 percent of these, accounting for 74 percent of the total value, were loans to traders. The next most important sectors were transport, manufacturing, and service and repair. It is interesting confirmation of the commercial bank attitude towards agriculture (and of the difficulty experienced by farmers in offering adequate security) that less than 2½ percent of the loans, corresponding to barely 3 percent of the total value, were for farming and livestock production. The banks have been notably reluctant to take advantage of the 100 percent guarantee, and in 1972 the Bank of Ghana, whose Development Finance Division was inadequately staffed to undertake the more thorough appraisal which would be advisable (because of the lending institution's refusal to accept any risk) had not yet pressed the banks to forward more proposals in this category. By May 1972, a 100 percent guarantee had been approved for only four loans.

Ghana's credit guarantee scheme has been described at some length because it is the only one to have been adopted in any of the countries in the present study, and because at least one other country (Kenya) has been considering whether a scheme should be introduced. Generally, it may be inferred from the Ghanaian experience that any such scheme, even if its application to certain categories of lending is compulsory, should at least offer the banks the incentive of a reasonable profit. In addition – and although in 1972 no information was available about the default rate on loans covered under the Ghanaian scheme – it seemed that it might be prudent to set aside a rather larger capital fund. The Ghanaian fund (₵2m at the end of March 1972) might all too easily be exhausted in a severe trade depression.

All three commercial banks are giving increasing attention to providing medium-term finance. In particular, Ghana Commercial Bank has a separate Development Financing Unit (DFU), staffed in mid-1972 by some seventeen professional officers, which makes loans (usually of ₵40,000 or more) for periods of up to five years. To some extent, the operations of the DFU overlap with those of the National Investment Bank, and this overlap might increase if (as was apparently being considered) the DFU were enabled to participate in equity and management. Alternatively, if NIB concentrated on larger projects (mainly covering longer periods), the DFU might be an increasingly important source of medium-term finance for Ghanaian business. At present, DFU's new loans amount to about ₵2–3m per annum. The major proportion of this is now granted to industrial enterprises. Apparently, substantially more than 50 percent of the total is lent to Africans, but detailed figures are not disclosed.

Expatriate Companies

It has already been noted that expatriate companies play an important role in import and export business, and directly or indirectly, Ghanaian traders depend heavily on them (and on GNTC) for supplies.

Until a few years ago, many Ghanaian traders used expatriate companies as their bankers. Each trader was issued with a passbook, in which his deposits were entered, and he was allowed to make credit purchases up to the value of his accumulated balance. But although the passbook system has provided an effective form of financial discipline, the United Africa Company's Tied Assisted Customers Scheme has been rather more significant in terms of active assistance. In 1960–61, UAC selected about twenty of its better-established passbook customers and leased them free premises, offered them unsecured credit, and gave them direct access to a sales manager who could advise on management and record-keeping. The Scheme has had some setbacks, notably – at times of import restrictions – when the Company was unable to meet all the demands of its tied customers; but it has gradually expanded, and by 1972 there were about 100 traders involved.

Several other companies have given limited amounts of credit and technical assistance to their Ghanaian distributors. In some cases they have acted as confirming houses to enable Ghanaian traders to import goods from overseas. A reverse complementarity has also applied, in so far as Ghanaian manufacturers have benefited from having their goods distributed by expatriate companies, and from having to conform with such companies' quality standards.

Conclusion

The prime requisite for the further development of Ghanaian entrepreneurship — outside relatively shady areas not amenable to direct government assistance — is the improvement of Ghana's general economic situation. Moreover, it would be unrealistic, given the present state of Ghanaian business development, to suppose that a better concerted effort to promote Ghanaian business would make an important contribution to overcoming the country's pressing economic problems. Therefore, the immediate prospects of Ghanaian businessmen can only be regarded with extreme pessimism.

Nevertheless, on the assumption that the climate does improve during the next couple of years, the Ghana government should now be working out a more coherent policy for the future. No real attempt yet seems to have been made, either to assess what degree of Ghanaian entrepreneurship already exists or to look beyond the conventional wisdom that the progress of Ghanaian entrepreneurs has been impeded merely by lack of capital and by ('unfair') alien competition. On the other hand, the design and implementation of more effective programmes of assistance would presuppose a better knowledge of what sort of people (and how many) the government was trying to help, together with a deeper understanding of the human and sociological problems involved. Even within the limits of the prevailing economic climate, it would also be necessary to review the more immediate business environment — including tax, licensing and other regulations — to see whether and to what extent this currently inhibits the response of entrepreneurs to whatever favourable opportunities do arise.

It seemed, therefore, that the most useful form of assistance which an outside agency could give in this field would be in high-level research and planning. One suitably experienced adviser, attached to the Ministry of Finance and Economic Planning, could at least recommend the framework for an economically more rational policy: a particularly important task would be to appraise the work of the Ghanaian Business Bureau and the Office of Business Promotion, with a view to suggesting which of these bodies should be given the central responsibility for co-ordinating future programmes.

Notes

1. P.C. Garlick, *African Traders and Economic Development in Ghana*, Oxford University Press, London, 1971.
2. Two of the Kumasi volunteers, Glenn Koehrsen and David Wagner, said in 1972 that they hoped to write a book based on their experiences.

Chapter 7 Kenya

Economic and Political Background

Kenya is a member, together with Uganda and Tanzania, of the East African Community. Primarily an agricultural country, Kenya also contains East Africa's main industrial centre (Nairobi) as well as the largest East African port (Mombasa), and it has a richer and more diversified economy than either of its East African partners.

Over the period 1964–71, Kenya's real gross domestic product grew at an average rate of between 6 percent and 7 percent per annum. It is provisionally estimated that Kenya's 1971 gross national product amounted to £K616m (equivalent to £660m Sterling). Shared between a population of about eleven million, this corresponds to a per caput income of about £60 Sterling; but this is a somewhat misleading figure since a substantial share of national income accrues to a small minority, many of whom (particularly outside government) are non-Africans. Kenya's population includes about 40,000 Europeans and 100,000 Asians.

The continuing improvement in purchasing power has given rise to an increasing demand for imports. Moreover, since a large proportion of Kenya's exports consist of agricultural products for which the world market is expanding comparatively slowly, Kenya faces a structural balance of payments problem. To some extent this was counteracted in the late 1960s by the inflow of long-term capital from abroad, but in 1971 there was a significant overall deterioration. In February 1972, the government introduced restrictions on many imports; and the 1972–73 budget was also relatively deflationary. In June 1972 it appeared that Kenya's post-independence economic boom was giving way to a mild recession. Since even during the boom period the modern wage sector was unable to absorb the annual increase to the labour force, this had worrying implications for the employment situation. Kenya already had a high degree of open and disguised unemployment.[1]

The Kenya government has consistently maintained a favourable attitude towards the private sector and continues to welcome foreign private investment. Nevertheless, there has been continuing emphasis on

'Kenyanisation', particularly of small- and medium-scale commerce. With regard to existing industry, notwithstanding some specific measures to promote new Kenyan industrial enterprise, the government seems to accept that for the time being its most realistic policy lies in localisation of expatriate staff rather than in transfers of actual ownership; but in the commercial sector, although the 1970—74 Development Plan lists the government's main objectives as efficiency, consumer protection, expansion, and Kenyanisation, in that order, the government has shown in its legislation and its day-to-day administration that a high priority is being given to Kenyanisation of ownership. In any case, the prime motivation for the whole Kenyanisation policy, in both commerce and industry, appears — at least until recently — to have been political and sociological rather than economic.

The Present State of African Entrepreneurship

There are no statistics to indicate the precise extent to which Africans are involved in non-agricultural business. During the colonial period, Kenya's non-agricultural private sector development was almost entirely financed by foreign (or at least non-African) investment. Management was also non-African in both commerce and industry. Wholesale and retail trade was predominantly controlled by Asians, although some large — mainly specialised — wholesale and import business had been developed by Europeans. Such African trading tradition as had grown up by the late nineteenth century — among the Kikuyu, for example — was effectively destroyed by Asian competition: the Kenya government estimates that as recently as 1966 only 30 percent of total wholesale and retail trade was controlled by Kenya citizens, and this proportion included an unspecified share controlled by citizens who were non-Africans. Marris and Somerset judged that in 1967 'there were scarcely 200 African businesses in Kenya larger than a country store or a craftsman's workshop, and even these few were still mostly small affairs'.[2] Although the African share of commerce, particularly of retail trade, has since increased, the overall African share of relatively large-scale business, particularly in industry, is undoubtedly still very small.

On the other hand, it is clear that non-agricultural African enterprises, however small they may be individually, have an important share in the economy. In 1969 an unpublished government survey estimated that there were nearly 40,000 small-scale African-owned

businesses operating in the rural areas: more than half of these were
retail traders, but others were engaged in a wide range of activities
including food services (about 10 percent), small-scale manufacture
(also nearly 10 percent), processing, repairs, and other services. No
corresponding survey has been made in the towns, but it is unofficially
estimated that the number of comparable small-scale enterprises in the
main urban areas, in the same year, may have been as many as 32,000.
The total employment, including self-employment, provided by all
small-scale African businesses may be more than half a million, which
would correspond to nearly half of Kenya's total non-agricultural
employment. Generally, African business appears to have been growing
fairly fast. But, particularly at the smaller-scale levels, this growth has
largely reflected the buoyancy of the national economy rather than the
success of any concerted attempt to provide government assistance.
Most of the small African businesses are not officially registered or
recognised, and many are not complying with minimum wage legislation, health standards, and other statutory obligations.

The 1972 ILO employment mission distinguished between the
'formal' and 'informal' sectors – the latter, including carpenters,
masons, cooks and taxi-drivers, 'offering virtually the full range of basic
skills needed to provide goods and services for a large though often
poor section of the population'. Within the time available for the
present study it was necessary to concentrate on African businessmen
already within or on the threshold of the formal sector. But it is
important that the ILO mission judged that 'the bulk of employment in
the informal sector ... is economically efficient and profit-making
though small in scale and limited by simple technologies, little capital
and lack of links with the other sector.' Moreover, although it required
considerable imagination to see the informal sector as one 'of thriving
economic activity and a source of Kenya's future wealth', such
imagination was not only 'necessary to solve Kenya's employment
problem' but also 'entirely called for' by the available evidence. The
mission urged the government to take a more positive attitude towards
promotion of the informal sector, and, in particular, to desist from
demolition of informal-sector housing (except where land was actually
required for housing development and town planning purposes), and
thoroughly to review the system of trade and commercial licensing,
preferably so as to eliminate all licensing of businesses in which there
was not clearly 'a reasonable and direct influence on health'. The
existing licensing system, which was not investigated in detail either by
the mission or in the present study, restricts the numbers of licences

issued, giving rise to monopoly profits for licence holders and also discouraging informal-sector investment because of the risk of police action against operators not holding licences.

Government Programmes of Assistance

Predominantly within the 'formal' sector, Kenya government agencies have between them instituted a remarkably wide range of measures or programmes which bear in some way on the development of private African entrepreneurship. But at least until recently these were for the most part poorly co-ordinated and, so far as positive promotion was concerned, the great majority of small African businessmen were hardly (if at all) affected. In February 1972 the Ministry of Finance and Planning appointed an informal inter-ministerial working party, to examine the existing institutions and to recommend a more effective organisational structure for assisting small Kenyan businessmen. In June of the same year the working party was still preparing its report, and although the working party's findings have not been made public, it was possible, on the basis of discussions with some of the officials concerned, to establish the main substance of the report's probable recommendations. If these recommendations are accepted and implemented, several of the criticisms contained in this chapter may become redundant.

The government's measures of discrimination against non-citizen businessmen were described in Chapter 3, and it was pointed out that, notwithstanding the operations of the Kenya National Trading Corporation, the delicensing of non-citizens has been insufficiently supported by practical assistance and advice to the Africans who have taken over their businesses. Nevertheless, in view of the deep entrenchment of the Asian community, there is no doubt that some degree of discrimination was an essential prerequisite for the improvement of business opportunities for Africans.

The main government loans schemes have also been outlined (Chapter 4). At the lower end of the scale, the District Joint Loan Boards, issuing loans of up to K£500, usually repayable over two to three years, are mainly concerned with enabling small traders to acquire stock. Loan money is contributed, on a fifty-fifty basis, by central government and County Councils; and in 1972 several of the 37 Boards were currently not operating because of the failure by the relevant local authorities to make their contribution. Loan disbursements are usually against supplier invoices, but the Boards have experienced heavy defaults, largely due to inadequate follow-up. From the beginning of 1965 to the end of 1971 a total of about K£900,000 was disbursed; in mid-1972 more than 20 percent of this amount was in default.

Much more significant, at least in terms of the total sums involved, are the schemes operated by the Industrial and Commercial Development Corporation. ICDC, an autonomous body under the Ministry of Commerce and Industry, was established, as the Industrial Development Corporation, in 1954. It was renamed in 1967. Since independence, while continuing to promote relatively large-scale ventures (mainly in partnership with foreign-owned capital) the Corporation has given increasing emphasis to facilitating African entry into what was previously an almost entirely alien or expatriate-dominated sector. ICDC's small business loans schemes have been such expanded, and the total volume of outstanding loans increased by K£74,000 (K£51,000 for commerce and K£21,000 for industry) in 1966–67, by K£620,000 (including small property loans and loans to tenants of Kenya Industrial Estates) in 1968–69, and by nearly K£1.7m in 1970–71. The increases in commercial and property loans have been particularly marked, together accounting for more than £1.3m of the increase during 1970–71, and it should therefore be noted that a large proportion of recent ICDC loans have merely been directed to enabling Africans to purchase businesses or premises from non-citizens.

The terms of ICDC loans were summarised in Table 3 (Chapter 4). With a loans department containing in 1972 about twenty professional staff, ICDC claims to place high priority on the thorough appraisal of loan applications. This has probably been an important reason for the fairly low rates of default which the schemes have experienced. On the other hand, ICDC has been widely criticised, especially by African industrialists who are not tenants of KIE, for its slow, bureaucratic procedures, and for the lack of understanding and sympathy shown by its staff to the needs of African businessmen. There have also been allegations that personal involvement in business by ICDC staff has threatened their impartiality, and that politicians and senior civil servants have used undue influence in obtaining loans for themselves, their associates, or their relatives. Appraisal procedures may be streamlined following the recent appointment of ICDC Provincial Officers, but ICDC borrowers could still benefit greatly from improved follow-up and advice. Although a special management services division (also now possessing a staff of about twenty) was set up in 1969, this has mainly been concerned with accounting and with the valuation (on behalf of prospective African purchasers) of non-citizen businesses. Marris and Somerset found that nearly two-thirds of the ICDC small borrowers whom they interviewed in 1966–67 felt a need for advisory services and practical training. The picture does not seem to have changed. In 1972 the Corporation still tended to react to any hint of default by concentrating on recovering its money rather than on trying to diagnose what had gone wrong.

A number of institutions do exist for giving training or advice, but they have been only partly concerned with the needs of African businessmen, and their work has not been co-ordinated with that of ICDC. So far as management training is concerned, however, it might appear – at least at first sight – that the Management Training and Advisory Centre is well fitted to take on a more important co-ordinating role. The MTAC, jointly financed by the Kenya government and UNDP, and employing an international team of experts recruited by the ILO, was established in 1966. At first, it concentrated almost exclusively on high-level management training and on consultancy work. In 1968, however, one of the ILO experts was given the responsibility of developing courses for self-employed African businessmen. Courses were run in Accounting, Marketing for New African Wholesalers, and simple Management Training (both for small traders and small manufacturers), and several were taken to centres outside Nairobi. Fees (in contrast with those charged for the more sophisticated management courses) were kept fairly low – Shs. 30 per course (usually for one week, but in some cases with follow-up consultancy). About 30 to 35 people attended each course.

Equipped with suitable personnel, the scheme might usefully be expanded, and expansion would be welcomed by African businessmen. In contrast, the MTAC's higher-level activities have not succeeded in attracting regular support, either from expatriate companies or from the public sector. A wide variety of courses and seminars for high- and middle-level management is now also offered by the Kenya Institute of Management, while the University of Nairobi's Faculty of Commerce provides management training, at both undergraduate and post-graduate level, to full-time students. In mid-1972, therefore, the government proposed, in line with recommendations contained in the Report of the Training Review Committee set up in 1971 under the chairmanship of W.N. Wamalwa, that the MTAC be converted into a Business Promotion and Advisory Centre (BPAC) concentrating entirely on the development of small-scale African entrepreneurship. It was envisaged that the BPAC become a focal point for all small-scale entrepreneurial and management training throughout Kenya. The Ministry of Finance's working-party, on the other hand, seemed to doubt whether the existing MTAC could undergo a sufficiently radical metamorphosis to become really effective in this new role. A further Wamalwa recommendation, that the Centre should become a responsibility of the Ministry of Commerce and Industry rather than the Ministry of Labour, had still not been implemented; and despite the success of the one expert, a New Zealander, who had developed the courses for African businessmen, and who was himself probably well fitted to adapt to a more extensive approach, it was doubtful whether ILO could design, staff, and implement an appropriate project, particularly in view of its bias towards relatively sophisticated management training.

Kenya possesses a wide range of institutions which provide technical training. Two polytechnics, in Nairobi and Mombasa, mainly concentrate on professional and technician training, while Nairobi's National Industrial Vocational Training Centre (NIVTC) is the country's principal centre for craft training. In 1972 there were eight secondary vocational schools, and four secondary technical schools, intended to prepare their pupils for further training rather than to turn out finished craftsmen and technicians. But particularly since the NIVTC and the polytechnics mainly cater for part-time students, who are usually sponsored by their employers, it is more important in the present context to consider the Kenya Industrial Training Institute, the Village Polytechnics, and the work (in promoting and assisting African building contractors) of the National Construction Corporation.

The Kenya Industrial Training Institute (KITI) was established in 1964 at Nakuru, with technical and financial assistance from Japan. Operating a one-year course for eighty students, who are required to possess a basic minimum level of technical skill before they can be accepted, KITI is particularly interesting in that, in addition to improving craft skills, it aims to give its trainees sufficient business training to enable them to be self-employed. Out of a total of 1509 course hours (1971 figures), 460 are devoted to business subjects, which include accounting, marketing, costing, and management of small enterprises. The Institute also provides a follow-up advisory service. Noting that this type of training could have a real impact on the unemployment problem, and that it could also facilitate the implementation of the government's Kenyanisation and rural development programmes, the Wamalwa Committee recommended that more institutes, similar to KITI, be established 'as soon as practicable'. Meanwhile, the existing Institute seems well fitted for greater national responsibility within the government's small business development programme.

At a lower level, and even more significant from the point of view of their low cost and their contribution to rural self-employment, are the Village Polytechnics (VPs). Initially sponsored by the National Christian Council of Kenya, with encouragement from the government, the first VPs were set up in 1966. Their main function is to teach basic technical skills to primary school leavers, to equip them for a more useful life within their local community. Emphasis is placed on community initiative and responsibility: each VP must have a local sponsor (a church or a county council, for example), who sees to the election of a local management committee. Construction and runnung costs are kept to a minimum, with recurrent cost per trainee of not more than about K£30 per annum. Curricula are supposed to be based on careful and regular survey of local needs. Subjects taught typically include carpentry, building, plumbing, mechanics, and tailoring, and each VP is being encouraged, where possible, to introduce a book-keeping programme. Trainees are not given any sort of diploma (such as might encourage them to migrate to the towns), and preliminary study suggests that nearly 70 percent of VP leavers take up employment or further training in rural areas.

By 1972 there were about 70 VPs, the majority of which were receiving financial support from the government. It was provisionally planned that there be 250 government-assisted VPs by 1978; but even this number could cater for only about 10–15 percent of primary school leavers. Moreover, it would not be easy, if the programme was expanded so rapidly, to improve standards of instruction (already rather unsatisfactory). Although as a basic principle the government must continue to rely on local initiative and management, it has an obvious direct responsibility to see that VPs are geared to the needs of the areas they serve. In 1972 the VPs were continuing to concentrate on training school leavers, mainly in non-agricultural skills. But in some areas it was already difficult for a specialised craftsman to find full-time employment, and it would be better if the VPs also equipped him to work as a part-time farmer. For this reason, and also to build and reinforce community attitudes towards integrated rural development, the VPs should in due course provide more agricultural training and, ceasing to be mainly restricted to training school leavers, they should become focal points for government and other programmes for promoting broader community development (ranging from adult literacy campaigns to agricultural extension services).

The National Construction Corporation (NCC), a joint venture
between the Kenya Government and the Norwegian aid agency,
NORAD, was set up in 1967 with the object of training indigenous
African contractors and enabling them to increase their share in the
national construction industry. Initially it was a private limited
company, but in 1972 it became (under the National Construction
Corporation Act) a statutory corporation. It has a total staff in 1972 of
about 60, including fourteen expatriates, and it principally operates by
allocating government and other contracts to Kenyan contractors, and
assisting them with short-term finance and on-the-job training. NCC's
principal client is the Ministry of Works, and government contracts of
up to K£20,000 are effectively reserved for NCC allocation. NCC
usually itself takes responsibility as main contractor, but work is
sub-contracted to Kenyan firms, selected by competitive tender or by
negotiation from the Corporation's approved list. (This list contains
about 900 firms, but only about 60 regularly receive NCC contracts.) In
1971, NCC issued 135 loans, valued at K£240,000. In addition to
providing on-site supervision and advice, NCC also ran 22 short courses
for African contractors.

NCC has been assisted in the design of its course material by a
non-profit-making London firm, Building for Development (BfD),
which is associated with the Intermediate Technology Development
Group. BfD's Research and Development Officer, Derek Miles, has
made a case-study of NCC, with recommendations for the improvement
of BfD's training function,[3] and for a thorough review of NCC lending
procedures. The Corporation's loans, often issued without any
security, carry interest of 8 percent and are usually repayable within
about six months; and (although no figure is mentioned in the BfD
report) the Corporation's bad debt ratio is believed, on the basis of
discussions with government officials, to be at least 20 percent. The
Corporation hopes to cut this to not more than 10 percent; but this
would not greatly reduce NCC's overall running costs. Administrative
expenses, which have risen sharply in the last three years, were
provisionally estimated at £225,000 for 1972/73.

NCC's ability to make loans has sometimes made it vulnerable to
political pressure, and the existence of a loans fund has encouraged
inexperienced businessmen to seek NCC contracts, thereby increasing
competition for the established firms and lessening their chances of
continuous employment. On the other hand, there is the paradox that
NCC has apparently sometimes favoured firms who have previously
defaulted on loan obligations, in the hope that the profit they earned

would enable the outstanding balance to be repaid. Despite these problems, it would be much harder for a project like NCC to make a useful impact if it was not able to provide financial assistance. A more fundamental criticism of NCC is that it has concentrated too much on technical aspects of construction, without giving its protégés sufficient training in financial and general management.

The various Kenya government programmes so far described have been listed in a necessarily rather piecemeal and disconnected fashion. As was explained earlier, there had been little attempt – at least until the Ministry of Finance and Planning's initiative in 1972 – to relate or co-ordinate programmes. There is, however, one particular group of entrepreneurs for whom the government has attempted to provide a better co-ordinated package of assistance – the entrepreneurs installed on KIE's first industrial estate. At the time of the appointment of the working party, the government not only proposed to build more industrial estates, but had also decided to make KIE responsible for the construction of a number of rural industrial development centres (RIDCs). The basic objectives of the rural industrial development programme (RIDP) were to be similar to those of KIE, except that the RIDP was to be specifically concerned with developing industry in rural areas. This policy would have strengthened the distinction between industrial promotion and other forms of small business development, and under KIE's direction the RIDCs were conceived as instruments for concentrating on fairly small groups of selected entrepreneurs. The working party, on the other hand, appeared to favour a broader and more extensive approach: the RIDCs should be centres for all small business development programmes and, as such, they should be a direct responsibility of KIE's parent, the ICDC. The remainder of this section is devoted to a discussion of KIE, the proposed RIDP, and the prospects for improved overall coordination, of all the services required by small businessmen, through ICDC. The section concludes with an examination of a business promotion programme, strictly speaking a private-sector project, which has been established in Kenya's Western Province by a US foundation, Partnership for Productivity.

The first phase of the Nairobi Industrial Estate was described in Chapter 5, and detailed information concerning costs and employment was listed in Table 4. Some of the problems which have been encountered, both by the entrepreneurs themselves and by KIE as a whole, were also discussed, and although some of these may now with the benefit of experience be overcome or, in subsequent projects, avoided, it was suggested that the construction of further estates ought to be preceded by more rigorous study and economic evaluation both of the Nairobi estate and of comparable estates elsewhere in Africa.

Nevertheless, it seemed in 1972 that the Kenya government was politically determined to go ahead with the KIE programme. At Nairobi, construction of the estate's second phase had been completed, and five of the 24 factory units were in operation. In view of the management and marketing problems experienced by some of the more ambitious projects in the first phase, one must have doubts on the viability of some of the new projects. The individual units are generally larger in area than those in the first phase (in the range 1,350–9,000 square feet, as compared to 625–3,750 square feet in Phase I), and although construction costs (per unit area) were expected to be less, the total cost of machinery and equipment, nearly K£½m, would be more than four times the amount required for Phase I. In addition, a completely new estate, consisting of about 21 units, is being construc- ted at Nakuru; and there are plans for at least three further estates, at Kisumu, Mombasa, and Eldoret.

Although the KIE programme directly assists only a very small number of Kenyan entrepreneurs, and despite its relatively small contribution to relieving the unemployment problem, the government working party apparently took the view that the development of further estates was to be encouraged. This conclusion may, however, have owed more to political than to economic considerations. It is more significant to the overall development of Kenyan entrepreneurship that the working party was convinced that the government should recon- sider its policy that KIE be responsible for the Rural Industrial Development Centres.

Compared to the KIE programme, the Rural Industrial Development Programme is more easily justified — in terms of its potential multiplier effects, as well as its prospective direct contribution to less centralised development and increased employment. Preliminary surveys have already been made for at least fourteen Centres. Construction of the first four Centres began in 1971, and was due for completion by the end of 1972; three of these (at Nyeri, Machakos, and Kakamega) have been financed by the Danish agency DANIDA, from which they are also receiving technical assistance, and the fourth (at Embu) has been given similar backing by NORAD. The government had also definitely approved in principle the establishment of a fifth Centre, at Kisii; but finance for this was still being sought.

Each RIDC consists of an administration block, a common facilities workshop (for use as a technical service centre as well as for demonstration and training), and a classroom. In addition, each Centre contains an area of open ground, temporarily left vacant, on which it would be possible to construct workshops for rental to selected entrepreneurs. The RIDC staff was initially to consist of a Kenyan manager, an expatriate technical adviser, a general mechanic, and one or two skilled trainers, chosen according to the needs of the area concerned. Each RIDC was to undertake feasibility studies of existing and possible local industries, to provide training, extension and repair services for small African industrialists and artisans, and to assist entrepreneurs to obtain loans from ICDC. The total capital cost associated with a single RIDC was estimated to be about K£95,000, made up as follows:

Construction	K£35,000
Machinery and equipment for common facilities workshop	20,000
Provision for loans to small industrialists	30,000
Staff housing	10,000
	95,000

In the case of the first four RIDCs, the external aid agencies concerned were providing this on a grant basis, and the Kenya government had undertaken to meet the local running costs, estimated at rather more than K£15,000 per Centre per year. The RIDC's headquarters staff consisted of a general manager, an expatriate technical adviser, and supporting clerical and secretarial staff, all accommodated in the administrative block of the Nairobi Industrial Estate.

From the point of view of developing small rural industry, it was obviously sensible that the RIDP should be closely associated with KIE. Specialised staff could then be shared, and the RIDCs have access to the Nairobi estate's under-utilised technical service centre, thus somewhat reducing their individual need for expensive and sophisticated equipment. Moreover, particularly with the KIE programme itself being expanded into new areas, it is clearly essential that the planning and administration of industrial estates and RIDCs should be closely co-ordinated. All this does not necessarily imply, however, that the RIDCs should be controlled by KIE. It would be equally satisfactory for both programmes to answer directly to ICDC. This arrangement would have the additional advantage that it would allow a reorientation of the RIDP's objectives and of the RIDCs' functions.

We have already noted that the various programmes of assistance to

Kenyan entrepreneurs have tended to operate too much in isolation from one another. This could give rise to increasing problems of duplication, but improved co-operation might permit the existing programmes to yield substantially greater benefits. More specifically, there is a widespread incapacity — shared by KIE, KNTC, and the National Construction Corporation, as well as by the ICDC and District Joint Board loan schemes — to meet the individual needs of African businessmen for managerial advice. Although the Ministry of Commerce and Industry has a field staff of some thirty Provincial and District Trade Officers, these have to devote much of their time to administrative duties, and their business promotion activity is largely limited to assisting African traders with book-keeping, and helping in the appraisal of loan applications.

Apart from the additional technical advice needed by the industrialist, the range of extension and other services characteristically required by the small African trader and the small African industrialist are broadly similar. It would greatly enhance the contribution of the RIDCs, therefore, if these were conceived as general centres for the co-ordination of all government assistance to small rural entrepreneurs. Larger businessmen, particularly those in the main towns, should of course continue to deal with ICDC and other agencies directly. The RIDCs, even under another name (Rural *Business* Development Centres, perhaps), would still need to employ some technical specialists, but the greater need, and one which would be a much greater problem, would be to recruit and train the extension staff who were competent on the one hand to recognise business opportunities and assist African businessmen to take advantage of them, and on the other to identify the problems of existing businessmen and assist in their remedy. Substantial external assistance would be required — not only to man the Centres themselves but also, more important in the long term, to assist in the training of local staff. It would also be necessary to give ICDC (on behalf of the Ministry of Commerce and Industry) unambiguous responsibility for all business development programmes. Unfortunately, ICDC as staffed and constituted is not a wholly appropriate institution for this task, and the government should commence with a thorough review of the Corporation's present operations and staff.

In its design of a more comprehensive business extension service, the Government will be able to profit from the experience of the pilot project which has been sponsored in the Kakamega District of Western Province by a new United States foundation, Partnership for

Productivity (PfP). First established at the end of 1970, in mid-1972 the project had eight senior staff members: three senior experts, three expatriate volunteers, and two Kenyans. All the expatriate staff were working for exceptionally low salaries, and PfP's total recurrent budget was therefore still no more than about K£35,000 per year.

Intensive managerial and technical assistance was being given to about eighteen Kenyan enterprises, ranging from a greengrocery and a small garage to a sawmill and a cloth printing company (which had been initiated, in co-operation with a selected entrepreneur, by PfP itself). About half of these had received small PfP loans: issued through a separate company, West Kenya Productivity Investments Ltd, these were mainly for periods of about one year, including a three-month grace period, and bore interest of 8½ percent per annum. The total sum involved was only about K£5,500. It is interesting, in view of what has been said elsewhere about the difficulties of lending to African businessmen that, despite the considerable attention devoted to these enterprises by PfP staff, the bad debts ratio was feared to be as high as 20 percent. PfP was also involved in a number of more general projects and activities including teaching at the local Village Polytechnic and the operation of a handicrafts shop.

PfP is widely acknowledged to be a unique and important experiment. Its staff are of a high calibre, and it would be exceedingly difficult to recruit larger numbers of similar expatriate personnel at comparable unit cost. A socio-economic evaluation of PfP's experiences was to be begun in late 1972 by a US post-graduate student in applied anthropology; and this, even if it confirms that realistically designed African business promotion programmes must be very expensive, might have a relevance to the development of African entrepreneurship in general. In any case the PfP experiment should be replicated elsewhere. Technically a private-sector project, it has been officially approved by the Kenya government to the extent that it is authorised to receive financial assistance direct from bilateral aid agencies. The Kakamega project is receiving backing ($40,000 in 1972/73) from USAID, which is also financing, in an area which overlaps that covered by PfP, a part of the Kenya government's Special Rural Development Programme. Another SRDP Division — at Kwale, near Mombasa — is being financed by Britain and this would seem to be a suitable area for another, probably rather smaller, PfP project, and, subject to request from the Kenya government, there are strong grounds for Britain at least to finance a feasibility study.

Commercial Banks

Kenya has a fairly diverse and well-developed commercial banking system, which includes three government-controlled commercial banks, a government-owned co-operative bank (mainly concerned with agriculture), three independent British banks and three Asian banks. The commercial banking system's total assets at 31 December 1970 were K£199m, of which K£87m constituted loans and advances. The banks wished to expand their lending but they had not been receiving enough reliably bankable proposals, and there had recently been moral suasion from the Central Bank not to increase their advances by more than about 1 percent per month, for reasons of overall economic policy.

There is little direct commercial bank lending to African commerce and industry. As in other countries, the African businessman is characteristically unable himself to finance either his fixed assets or his working capital: even where he is able to obtain medium- or long-term finance from ICDC, or from elsewhere, he usually cannot offer his bank acceptable security for a loan for working capital. Moreover, irrespective of the merits of his own proposal, he inevitably suffers from the poor reputation – as borrowers – of African businessmen as a group. The banks have themselves recently been under an additional constraint, arising from government pressures to accelerate the localisation of their expatriate staff. Many African branch managers have had little time to acquire experience; and their head-offices are correspondingly reluctant to encourage them to pursue a more adventurous lending policy.

Not surprisingly, the banks have found it easier to lend to ICDC. By 1972 there had been two consortium loans, of which the second (K£470,000) was devoted to the small loans schemes. Barclays Bank International and the Kenya Commercial Bank have both made separate additional loans (K£500,000 and K£750,000 respectively) for the same purpose of on-lending to African businessmen.

The 1970–74 Development Plan announced the introduction of a credit guarantee scheme, under which 'ICDC will guarantee the repayment of loans by businessmen whom the banks consider marginal cases and whose applications they would reject under their normal criteria'. It was proposed that 'a small commission' would be charged, both to the borrowers and the banks. In mid-1972, a precise scheme had still to be worked out. But the government working party was known to have had informal discussions on the subject with at least one of the expatriate-owned banks, and it was hoped that some arrangement might be reached whereby the government (probably through ICDC) would be able to guarantee up to about 75 percent of any commercial bank loan made to an African businessman. Initially, the scheme might apply only to loans to manufacturers. In any case, in the interests of the scheme's success, it was important that all the banks should be fully consulted at an early stage, and the scheme should not (like its counterpart in Ghana) be so designed as to make commercial bank lending to African business much less profitable than other forms of lending.

Expatriate Companies

Kenya has no individual expatriate company comparable in size to the United Africa Company in Ghana; but, particularly if one includes the large Asian firms, the expatriate private sector as a whole is relatively even more prominent in the economy.

Many firms have networks of African agents. Some firms have passed on some of their less technical overseas agency business to Africans, while the oil companies, notably Kenya Shell, provide training courses, with practical follow-up, for their tied dealers. In 1967 Kenya Shell also published a handbook, with side-by-side translations of English and Swahili, entitled 'How to Run a Business': this has since been re-issued in a metric version. Generally, however, 'assistance' to African businessmen only occurs where it is in the mutual interests of both parties. As in the case of the commercial banks, a more active role could only be expected if governments, in Kenya or Britain (the principal investing country), made it worthwhile. At present, moreover, most companies would be particularly reluctant, in view of the increasing government pressures to Kenyanise their remaining expatriate personnel, to assist with training programmes which are not strictly geared to their own needs.

Conclusion

African entrepreneurs in Kenya have the advantage of operating in an expanding economy. Up to now, government policy-makers have mainly been concerned to devise measures which can make it easier for Africans to obtain a larger share in the country's growing prosperity through becoming more truly integrated within the alien and expatriate-dominated 'formal' sector. For the future, particularly from the point of view of generating employment, it is perhaps even more important for the government to adopt a more positive approach towards 'non-formal' activities, and (for example, by encouraging subcontracting) seek to develop links which can steadily draw the two sectors more closely together.

As in other countries, the government is remarkably ill-informed about the nature and scale of the existing African private sector. But quite apart from the need for better statistics, there is also a special need to reappraise, from the point of view of the small African businessman, the effects of the many statutory and other regulations (including licensing restrictions) under which the private sector has to operate. Particularly in the urban areas, small African businessmen are constrained by a legal and institutional framework (largely a colonial inheritance) with which they can hardly hope to comply.[4] It is therefore essential to any wider government attempt to foster African entrepreneurship that the activities of small entrepreneurs at least be legalised. This is not to say that all standards should be removed or lowered: it might be possible, perhaps through some form of discriminatory licensing, to maintain existing standards in the urban centres but at the same time allow much more scope for small artisan and service enterprises in the less affluent suburbs.

Of the four countries included in the present study Kenya is perhaps the most interesting, by reason of the wide variety of African business promotion programmes in which the government has already engaged. The government has notably failed to co-ordinate the different programmes; but by mid-1972 there was the prospect of improvement if the recommendations of the government working party were accepted. Meanwhile, the individual experience, particularly of Kenya Industrial Estates, Kenya Industrial Training Institute, the National Construction Corporation, the Village Polytechnics, and, of course, the Industrial and Commercial Development Corporation, can be particularly valuable to governments contemplating comparable initiatives elsewhere. Subject to sufficient external support Kenya can continue its innovative role through the Rural Industrial Development Programme, which should be reformulated to include the development of all non-agricultural African entrepreneurship outside the urban areas.

The diversity of programmes partly reflects the interest and support of external donors. So far as Britain is concerned, total gross aid to Kenya amounts to some £11m per annum, and it is unlikely that Kenya would wish to switch a significant proportion of this to the finance of business promotion. But Britain could make a small but useful contribution by financing a Partnership for Productivity project in the Kwale special rural development area. Generally, Kenya's experiments deserve to be well studied, both by African government and by donors including Britain who might give assistance in this field to other African countries.

Notes

1. Kenya was selected for study by the third ILO-sponsored international employment mission. The mission visited Kenya between March and May 1972, and its report, *Employment, Incomes and Equality*, was published by ILO later in 1972.
2. Peter Marris and Anthony Somerset, *African Businessmen* Routledge and Kegan Paul, London, 1971.
3. *The National Construction Corporation, Kenya: a Study of an African Contractor Training Organisation*, BfD Information Paper no. 7, April 1972.
4. The ILO report noted that a district health inspector in North-East Province found himself issued with 'the same inspection manual as that used in London, containing regulations on such subjects as minimum temperatures for factories'.

Chapter 8 Malawi

Economic and Political Background

In terms of income per head, Malawi is the poorest of the countries included in this study. In the first seven years following independence (1964), real gross domestic product grew at an estimated annual rate of 5.9 percent; but in 1971 GDP still amounted to only 319 million Kwacha (equivalent to £160m), of which K119m (37 percent of the total) was the estimated product of the non-monetary sector. Gross national product was K313m: shared between an estimated population of 4.6m (increasing by at least 2½ percent per annum), this corresponds to GNP per caput of less than K70 (£35).

Malawi is predominantly an agricultural country, with 90 percent of the population living in rural areas, and the government is giving top priority to agricultural development.[1] Total wage employment is still barely 200,000 of which about one-third is in agriculture. There are (very approximately) an additional 200,000 Malawians working in Rhodesia, and a large but incalculable number working elsewhere in Southern Africa. Throughout the last fifty years, a substantial proportion of relatively enterprising Malawians have thus considered their best opportunities to lie outside Malawi itself: many still send money home, and their total remittances may be as much as K5m per annum.

The government has maintained a consistently favourable attitude towards the private sector, and foreign investment, so long as it is consistent with Malawi's development strategy, is generally welcomed. The government believes that industrial and commercial development must continue to depend heavily on foreign capital, but the state-owned Malawi Development Corporation (MDC) participates in many of the larger ventures, and the first steps have been taken to increase the Malawian share in smaller-scale enterprises, particularly in rural trading. With regard to the latter, it is acknowledged, more frankly than by most other African governments, that 'Any attempt at structural change must cause a temporary dislocation in services' and that 'it will be some time before Malawians are able to take full advantage of the commercial opportunities opened up to them'.[2]

The Present State of African Entrepreneurship

With the notable exception of some of the companies controlled by
Press Holdings (see below), non-agricultural Malawian private enterprise
is very poorly developed, and still largely confined to small-scale
commerce, so much so that many Malawians seem to interpret the
terms 'Malawian businessmen' and 'small trader' as virtually synony-
mous. There are more than 4,000 African shopkeepers, including some
relatively large ones in Northern Malawi (a part of the country in
which, during the colonial period, trading licences were not issued to
Asians, and where Mission education was developed earlier than
elsewhere). There are also a few African wholesalers (including about
five in the main commercial centre, Blantyre); but apart from the
operations of the government wholesaler (initially, in 1968, part of the
National Trading Company, since superseded by the Import and Export
Company), wholesaling is still predominantly in European and Asian
hands. Even with regard to retail trade, it was estimated as recently as
1967, that although probably 80 percent of the country's retail
licence-holders were African, these retailers together accounted for less
than 10 percent of the total volume of retail trade.

Apart from small craftsmen and a few builders, brickmakers, and
small timber operators, there are two other fields in which some degree
of Malawian entrepreneurship is relatively well established. These are
maize milling and motor transport. There are about 3,000 maize mills
scattered through the country and several hundred Malawian-owned
lorries. In 1971 the Malawi Road Transport Authority (MRTA), an
officially recognised and favoured body which for some years had been
closely and inefficiently co-ordinating a large part of Malawian road
transport operations, was finally closed down; the more efficient
operators have certainly benefited from their increased autonomy.
Following the discontinuation, in April 1971, of a long-established
expatriate monopoly, Malawians are now also permitted to operate bus
companies. Although the expatriate company, United Transport
(Malawi), has continued to operate much the largest fleet (more than
180 buses), by 1972 five locally-owned companies had been established
and were providing fairly effective competition on the major routes.
The government's 1972 Economic Report judged that service to
customers had improved as a result. In any case, the nature of the

response to this new business opportunity indicates that the Malawian capacity for entrepreneurship – including access to capital – may have been under-rated.

In this connection, it should also be noted that there is an active and expanding African Businessmen's Association, which by mid-1972 had nearly 1,000 members. Most of these operate in one or more of the fields already mentioned, and the great majority are small storekeepers. But a few essentially self-made men have built up quite large shops, with several paid employees, or are running fairly sophisticated enterprises as, for example, electrical contractors, brickmakers, dry cleaners, or caterers, or even (in one case) as a manufacturer of farm-carts. The owners of these larger businesses have generally spent some time abroad, usually in Rhodesia or South Africa, where they have accumulated their starting capital and also, equally important, acquired basic and technical skills and the ability to recognise business opportunities. Through their Association, they lament the lack of facilities for basic commercial training and the government's reluctance to discriminate in their favour by, for example, giving preference to African contractors. Their main concern, however, is that the government should promote more and better opportunities for African trade.

In view of the extreme inexperience of most Malawian businessmen, the government has probably been wise to concentrate its initial promotion efforts on the small African trader. Parts of Malawi (when it was Nyasaland) were among the last areas in Africa to come under any European or Asian influence, and in the absence of any indigenous entrepreneurial tradition it was natural that, when the Europeans and Asians (other than the first missionaries) did arrive, they should assume and maintain an effective monopoly over the slow growth of internal trade. Malawian education also developed very slowly, and although opportunities of education and training have at last been rapidly expanded, this expansion has largely been directed at localisation of the civil service, with the next priority being localisation of personnel in the existing expatriate private sector. School curricula are gradually being reoriented, but primarily to turn out better farmers, and commercial training (except for the rather sophisticated business studies courses offered by the Polytechnic) continues to be largely ignored. Better educated Malawians still seek first the prestige, security, and material benefits of a job with the government. Business, except as a side-interest, tends to be regarded only as a last resort. People with the education, capacity and confidence to organise any business bigger than a small store, still have little difficulty in finding paid employment – if not with government, then with one of the large private sector employers.

Several politicians and civil servants have been expanding their part-time business interests; but these, if they are not in small-scale commerce, are most often in agriculture. There is one indigenous group of companies, however, which is operating on a large scale in both agriculture and commerce. This is Press Holdings, a rapidly diversified conglomerate which is principally owned, on behalf of the Malawi Congress Party, by the Life President, Dr. Banda. The group's investments include tobacco farms, supermarkets, a department store, and a substantial share in the National Bank of Malawi. Although technically within the private sector, Press Holdings has effectively established itself as an alternative instrument to MDC for the purposes of local participation in foreign enterprises. It has the advantage of political preference and is obviously in a privileged position to borrow local money; but there is some doubt whether its management is fully competent to take on additional responsibilities. Some external observers were clearly worried, by mid-1972, that the group might already have expanded too fast, and in particular relied too much on loan finance.

Government Programmes of Assistance

The immediate objective of the government's business promotion programme has so far merely been to Africanise the existing system of rural distribution. It was appreciated that rapid replacement of Asians and Europeans by relatively inexperienced and under-capitalised Africans was liable to conflict with a broader government commitment – in furtherance of the general rural development effort – to improve distribution and stabilise prices, and responsibility for avoiding or minimising such a conflict has been given to the state-owned Import and Export Company. This Company only commenced operations in July 1971; in order to place it in its proper context it will be necessary to sketch the two-year history of its predecessor, the National Trading Company. There will also be reference to the government's legislation and policy (already discussed in Chapter 3) on trade licences; but first, since historically their foundation preceded by some ten years the formation of the National Trading Company, we should briefly refer to the national Loans Boards.

The details of Malawi's small business loans scheme have already been described (in Chapter 4: see Table 3). The African Loans Board was originally established in the 1950s. Loans were usually issued for three to five years, and the maximum size of loan (which might be exceeded, however, subject to Ministerial approval) was K1,000. During most of the 1960s there were two separate Boards, administering funds for agricultural and business loans respectively. In 1969 these were re-amalgamated, to form the Central Loans Board; but this has largely been concerned with trying to recover amounts outstanding, and very few business loans have been made since about 1967. The total size of the business loan fund was apparently never more than K170,000 (of which more than K40,000, together with accumulated interest of about K10,000, was still owing in mid-1972), and the fund was therefore never large enough to be of much economic significance. In any case, the approval procedure was subject to heavy political influence; it appears that many loans were granted primarily to reward deserving members of the Malawi Congress Party for their contribution to Malawi's attainment of independence. The Boards are relevant to the present study, therefore, only in so far as they exemplify the subordination of economic to political criteria.

The National Trading Company (NTC) is of more unique interest, since it is believed to represent the only attempt by an African government to design and implement a large-scale African business promotion programme with the help of a private expatriate-controlled company. It is significant that within two years the experiment broke down: the government became impatient at what they considered a slow rate of progress, whereas the expatriate partner (who still had a substantial equity shareholding) found that it would not be possible to satisfy the government's ambitions without seriously prejudicing NTC's profitability. (The government also expected NTC to be profitable but, compared to NTC, it was more optimistic about the prospective viability of some of its proposals.)

NTC was set up at the end of 1968, when MDC took a 51 percent shareholding in the largest expatriate trading company, Bookers (Malawi), the possessors of *inter alia* a nation-wide chain of wholesale and retail outlets. Bookers continued to manage the new Company, but the Board was reconstituted under a Malawian Chairman and a policy was formulated for the nation-wide promotion of African trade. In the course of the next two years, wholesale services were substantially improved, through the establishment of a chain of 26 wholesale depots, and credit facilities were granted (for an average amount of about K40 each) to about 200 traders. In addition, a personal advisory service was set up in 1969, and supplemented by a weekly radio programme, launched in June 1970, and the publication of a small book, 'Good Shopkeeping'.

Meanwhile, the government amended the Business Licensing Act to allow the exclusive reservation of rural areas, and some of the smaller trading centres, for Malawian trade (see Chapter 3). The issue and renewal of all non-Malawian trading licences had already been centralised in the Ministry of Trade and Industry, with effect from the beginning of 1969; this had enabled certain non-Malawians suspected of sharp practices to be forced out of business without resort to legislation. As from 1 July 1970, however, no non-Malawians were permitted to trade in rural areas.

Around the time that the new licensing restrictions became effective, there was already political disenchantment with NTC's allegedly slow progress and high prices. Although the Asians were withdrawing to the main urban areas, African traders now found themselves in competition with NTC, and it was particularly resented that NTC had not expanded credit as quickly as had been hoped. Accordingly, the government renegotiated its agreement with Bookers, and took complete ownership of NTC's assets in the rural areas in return for slightly more than half its NTC shares. Majority control of NTC, which was re-named Bookers (Malawi), thus returned to Bookers.

These rural assets, together with the responsibility for promoting African trade, have been vested since July 1971 in the Import and Export Company of Malawi (IECM), a wholly-owned subsidiary of MDC. IECM also took over about 360 of NTC's former staff, and new senior management was recruited from overseas. In its first few months, IECM established four new wholesale depots (taking the total number up to thirty) and also branched into new areas — first by taking over expatriate firms in the textile, electrical, pharmaceutical and motor trades, and then by building up a wide-ranging agency business. 1972 was largely a period of consolidation, and it remains to be seen whether IECM will be more successful than NTC in reconciling its principal objectives, which are to foster African trade, improve the distribution infrastructure (as a preconditional stimulus for farmers to increase their cash crop production), and make enough profit to finance further expansion. The Company already relies on bank overdrafts and export credits for its working capital, and one must sympathise with a management which is under political pressure to stabilise prices and at the same time accelerate the development of its own credit facilities.

On the other hand, IECM has the advantage compared to NTC that it has been given some important monopolies. In 1972 these included the distribution of sugar, hoes, and matches (which are all locally manufactured and subject to official price control) and the import of second-hand clothing and light-grade iron sheets. Moreover, provided that the Company's specialised divisions can generate a reasonable profit, it can afford merely to break even on its general trading operations.

Overall, it appeared in June 1972 that IECM had made a promising start. But this owed a great deal to the energy and ability of IECM's managing director and to a small, mainly expatriate, cadre of senior managers. Consolidation was certainly required. In particular, it was difficult to maintain adequate controls at lower levels (for example, over the management of the rural wholesale depots); credit facilities had been greatly expanded, to the extent that the average amount outstanding, from about 250 traders, was now nearly K800; and, although it was still maintained that IECM's operations in any field would only be continued until such time as African businessmen were competent to take over, the Company had still to institute an appropriate training programme. In theory IECM was itself to provide a training ground, particularly through its retail outlets, but first priority, understandably enough, was given to training the Company's own personnel. It would of course be possible for IECM to transfer its businesses to its own middle-level employees, and it might be easier to do this than to select and train African businessmen from within the private sector. On the other hand, it is not clear that this is what senior Malawian staff would want. It is all too easy to envisage that IECM could gradually expand, while yielding relatively few additional benefits to existing African businessmen. Particularly if the Company's key expatriates were prematurely replaced by inexperienced Malawians, IECM could become a large and inefficient bureaucracy whose staff were primarily concerned with the importance and security of their own jobs.

For IECM to be an effective instrument for helping existing African businessmen, it is probably necessary that it devote more resources to assisting traders on their own premises. Although a few short courses have been run for small groups of relatively sophisticated businessmen, notably by the Polytechnic (a constitutent College of the University) and by the Junior Chamber of Commerce, there is no institution in Malawi which regularly provides basic training of the sort which African traders need. It is obviously desirable, in the interests of IECM itself as well as of its clients, that trade credit be supported by a follow-up advisory service. It should be possible, perhaps with expatriate help, to train Malawians in the fairly simple teaching techniques which would be involved.

Apart from the responsibilities which we have already discussed, IECM has a general mandate to give preference to overseas suppliers who undertake to consider manufacturing their products within Malawi once a viable internal market has been established. IECM is also intended, in association with overseas partners where possible, to promote the development of Malawian industry and export markets for Malawian production. In pursuit of these objectives, and although in June 1972 IECM's Industrial and Export Division had still not been properly established, the Company wished to establish a small-scale industrial estate at Liwonde, which is strategically situated in the middle of the southern part of the country, at the intersection of the main north-south trunk road with the railway line to the Mozambique port of Nacala. It was envisaged that, for the project to be worthwhile, it would be necessary to start with at least five or six different industries, each of which would initially be a joint venture between IECM (or MDC) and a foreign investor, with provision for IECM's share, or an additional third share, to be purchased in due course by a Malawian entrepreneur. Possible products include agricultural machinery, tins, pills, rulers and pencils, and cotton wool. However MDC's Projects Division has still not been able to commence the necessary feasibility studies. Plans are therefore still vague, but it seems to be appreciated that the basic viability of any industry should be based on the Malawi market alone. Despite theadvantage of Malawi's unusual geo-political position and the possibility of developing trade with both white and black Africa, it would be dangerous to rely on exports to neighbouring countries.

IECM also hoped to construct a major distribution depot within the same complex. The total cost of infrastructure and buildings, including the factories, was provisionally estimated at K300,000 (£150,000), which would need to be externally financed. First, however, the whole proposal should be subjected to a thorough economic study. Attention should also be paid to the experience of comparable projects elsewhere. In the range of its products, the Liwonde estate would be more akin to the Nairobi estate than to the SEDCO estates in Swaziland (which do have the advantage of guaranteed external and tourist markets), but the Liwonde project is also different from either in that it seeks the direct involvement of foreign private investors. Even if some of IECM's suppliers could be induced to set up at Liwonde, it is doubtful whether they would countenance the rapid transfer, of both control and management, to local interests. In the absence of such transfer, on the other hand, the Liwonde project could not contribute to the development of African entrepreneurship.

It has already been emphasised that Malawi's education system is not designed to produce people suited for self-employment outside the agricultural sector. This applies both to formal education (including some twelve secondary schools which are now equipped with technical wings) and to most of the specialised institutions such as the Polytechnic and the country's five trade or technical schools. An additional Rural Trade School (RTSS) was opened in 1971 at Salima, on Lake Malawi, as part of an agricultural regional development project supported by West Germany. With an annual intake of about 60, this offers two-year courses for rural craftsmen, in simple building techniques (including carpentry) and basic metalwork. Like Kenya's Industrial Training Institute, RTSS includes commercial subjects in its curriculum (though on a less ambitious scale than the KITI) in order to prepare its trainees for self-employment.

Commercial Banks

Malawi has two commercial banks. The larger in terms of deposits is the National Bank of Malawi, a joint venture formed in July 1971 through a merger of the Malawi interests of Barclays and Standard. 49 percent of the equity was made available to government nominees, and the shareholders are Barclays Bank International (25½ percent), Standard Bank (25½ percent), Press Holdings (29 percent), and the Agricultural Development and Marketing Corporation (20 percent). The second bank, the Commercial Bank of Malawi, is also a joint venture, between a Portuguese commercial bank (60 percent) and MDC (40 percent). Despite its relatively small share of total business, and the fact that it was only established in April 1970, the Commercial Bank by 1972 already had more points of representation – nearly 80 (including agencies), compared to the 55 possessed by the National Bank. The Commercial Bank has thus made an important contribution to widening the availability of banking services; but it is believed to have made fairly heavy operating losses (in 1972 still undisclosed) in the process.

Malawi's banks have an unusually high ratio of advances to deposits. By March 1972 total loans and advances had reached K31.9m, compared to total deposits of K42.7m (corresponding to an advances/ deposits ratio of nearly 75 percent); and in mid-1972, at the instigation of the banks themselves and with only rather reluctant agreement from the government, non-priority advances (particularly to commercial borrowers) were being reduced. African businessmen were only indirectly affected, however. The great majority of bank lending has been to expatriate or non-African enterprises, and to the public sector; and although seasonal advances to African farmers have gradually been expanding, there is very little lending to African traders. Adequate security is not usually available; and, more fundamentally, on the basis of their limited experience the banks regard the African businessman as a bad risk.

There have been no plans for the official guarantee of commercial bank credits, and, given the present state of African business development, it is unlikely that a credit guarantee scheme could usefully be introduced in the near future. There might be better prospects of developing African business through contribution by the banks to a single indigenous institution, with special staff. But this would probably need an operating subsidy, and the success of its operations might be severely prejudiced by political influence.

Expatriate Companies

The NTC experiment, involving the Malawi subsidiary of the London firm Booker McConnell, was described earlier in this chapter. As in other countries, some expatriate companies (including Bookers) are providing useful training to African businessmen through the regular visits of their merchandisers and salesmen, and at least two companies have introduced schemes whereby selected traders are consigned with particular amounts of stock, which are sold by the trader on a commission basis and, so long as the trader keeps a regular bank account and maintains proper records, replenished by the supplier. Generally, however, Malawi's expatriate companies, many of whom are controlled from white Southern Africa, appear to be more parochial and less enlightened (even in what might appear to be their long-term self-interest) than their counterparts in economically larger African countries further north.

Conclusion

The best prospects for the further development of Malawian private enterprise lie in the continued expansion of the Malawian economy; and, assuming that the official optimism concerning export markets is justified, present government policy, of concentrating on increasing agricultural production, should yield important benefits in other sectors. Moreover, in view of the mutually reinforcing advantages of improving the structure and efficiency of rural distribution, and also because such a high proportion of Malawian businessmen are traders, it is also sensible that the government should concentrate its principal efforts, directly to promote African business, on the commercial sector. Even so, IECM should undertake a more definite training programme, both as a means to improving trading services and to equip businessmen with the basic commercial knowledge which can make it easier for them to branch out into other fields.

The government should also seek to improve its knowledge of the degree of African entrepreneurship which already exists in Malawi, both in shopkeeping and in other sectors. The IECM was planning to conduct, late in 1972, a preliminary survey of Malawian traders: even if the National Statistical Office could not spare the resources for a more professional exercise, the African Businessmen's Association would at least be able to assist in building up a more comprehensive picture of the state of Malawian entrepreneurship within the 'formal' sector (to borrow the terminology adopted by the ILO mission to Kenya). In addition, the government should further review formal education curricula, to see whether simple commercial training could be made more widely available at an earlier stage. Finally, as in most other African countries, there needs to be a critical reappraisal of the whole business environment, including an examination of 'informal' enterprise, and how this can be more closely linked to the rest of the economy.

Some of this survey work would benefit from foreign technical assistance. Otherwise, except for the need to examine more closely the proposal to establish a small industrial estate at Liwonde, and technical assistance to IECM, it is difficult to see how external agencies could significantly contribute, in the foreseeable future, to Malawian private-sector development. The government would certainly wish any aid in this area to be additional to what it was already receiving, and it is therefore particularly unlikely that it would (or could) welcome such aid from Britain.

Notes

1. For a general description of Malawi Government policy, see
   Statement of Development Policies 1971–1980, prepared by the
   Economic Planning Division of the Office of the President and
   Cabinet and published in December 1971.
2. Ibid., p. 4.

Chapter 9 Swaziland

Economic and Political Background

One of the three former so-called High Commission territories, Swaziland (together with South Africa, Botswana, and Lesotho) continues to be a member of the Southern African Customs Area. The development of the modern economy, which has been almost entirely financed by foreign private investment and official aid, is remarkably diverse for such a small country (6,700 square miles, with a total population of less than half a million), but it has largely been restricted to a few relatively small centres of economic activity, and the majority of the population still maintains a subsistence way of life in the rural areas. Gross domestic product in 1967/68 (the latest year for which figures are available) is estimated to have been R50.6m (£29.5m), of which 29 percent was in agriculture, 20 percent in mining and construction, and 13 percent in manufacturing, mainly first-stage processing of local primary products. Gross national product was R45.5m, corresponding to more than £55 per head; but the latter figure is somewhat misleading. The actual amount paid out in wages and salaries was R26.3m, and a significant proportion of this must have accrued to 'Europeans', including white South Africans who comprise about 3,000 of the country's 50,000 wage employees. It is not yet possible to estimate the rate of Swaziland's recent economic growth, but the rapid expansion of the cash economy has been reflected in a spectacular increase in the value of the country's exports – from R12m in 1960, to R40m in 1967 and about R54½m in 1971. (The 1967 figure, when compared to the 1967/68 GDP figure already quoted, also indicates the extent to which the economy is oriented towards external trade.)

Swaziland became independent in 1968. The Post Independence Development Plan stated that the government's main development objective was 'to improve the living conditions of the mass of the people'.[1] Particularly high priority would be given to the development of agriculture and related industries. At the same time, the government continued to look to the private sector to spearhead economic development and would encourage 'a continued substantial

95

inflow of foreign capital in agriculture, mining, industry, commerce and other business'. It was thus acknowledged that the continued growth of the monetary economy depends heavily on foreign private investment. Simultaneously a 'special effort' would be made 'to promote small local businesses'. Government hoped, thereby, to do four things: to lessen Swaziland's dependence on South African suppliers of essential consumer goods; to stimulate further processing, within Swaziland, of secondary materials produced by the country's larger enterprises; to lessen the dualistic nature of the economy; and – by spreading wage-earning opportunities to new locations – to check the drift of the rural population, especially young people, to the main urban areas.

The Present State of African Entrepreneurship

African entrepreneurship is mainly confined to small-scale commerce. Trading licences are still administered at the district level, and detailed statistics are not available, but it is estimated that there are nearly 600 Swazi traders, of which 90 percent run general stores, 8 percent are butchers and the remaining 2 percent (mainly in towns) have other specialised sorts of business. Very few stores are formally owned by Asians, since few Asians were allowed to settle in Swaziland, but a number of Swazi-owned stores are effectively controlled by Asians (usually wholesalers with whom Swazi storekeepers have run into debt) living in South Africa. The main trading centres are largely dominated by European businesses, and there are also some large European-owned stores in the rural areas. There are no private Swazi wholesalers.

There are a number of Swazi entrepreneurs in small, mainly handicraft-type, industries. Most of these are associated with the Small Enterprises Development Company (SEDCO). In May 1972 there were about fifty entrepreneurs, a small proportion of whom were not Swazi, installed on SEDCO estates; and SEDCO was also giving advice or assistance to about twelve Swazi contractors. The only other field in which Swazi entrepreneurship is fairly well established is road transportation, particularly bus services. The Road Transportation Board estimates that in December 1971 scheduled passenger services were being provided by no less than 128 operators, nearly all Swazi, who between them owned a total of 242 vehicles, most of them mini-buses.

Government Programmes of Assistance

The first attempt at encouraging Swazi entrepreneurship was made by the traditional government. In 1946 the King, wishing to promote wise investment of savings accumulated by Swazi serving in the war, founded an association called the Swazi Commercial Amadoda. Despite intermittent enthusiasm to use it as an instrument for encouraging business co-operation, this body has generally been inefficiently run and, except for some contribution to Swazi progress in the transportation sector, has had little impact. Otherwise, apart from spasmodic and generally rather unsuccessful efforts to improve and co-ordinate the rural handicrafts industry (in a way which, in any case, tended to lessen the degree of entrepreneurial initiative required from the individual producer), the government has only recently become involved in actively promoting Swazi entrepreneurship.

The Swaziland programme is particularly notable for two reasons: first, it was originally conceived in order to promote small productive enterprises as well as Swazi commerce; and second, because of Swaziland's small size it was able, fairly quickly, to make a perceptible economic and political impact. Unfortunately, its political importance may be its undoing. Having been supported from the start by an unusually energetic Minister, responsible for both commerce and industry, in mid-1972 the programme was threatened by a government reorganisation which transferred commerce to a new portfolio held by another Minister, with whom the first, still responsible for industry, would not find it easy to co-operate. It was still not exactly clear how the programme would be divided, nor how its co-ordination or prospective viability would be affected.

Basically, the programme is a joint venture between the government (who financed most of its capital contribution from British official loans) and the ILO. The UNDP/ILO project, which is to last three years, did not formally commence until March 1972. But the first British aid money was requested in 1969, and the ILO chief of project, who largely designed the project and made an exploratory visit to Swaziland as early as 1968, was himself working in Swaziland by the middle of 1970. Initially, three inter-related organisations were established; and these — the Small Enterprises Promotion Office, the Small Enterprises Development Company, and Swazi Craft — were staffed by a combination of local personnel, UN experts, and volunteers. Many individuals worked for two or three of these institutions simultaneously; in addition, two previously existing bodies, the Swazi

Commercial Amadoda and the Swaziland Credit and Savings Bank, have been closely associated with the programme; and the Small Enterprises Development Company and the Commercial Amadoda have been joint shareholders in another new venture, Amadoda Distributors, designed to provide an improved wholesaling service for Swazi traders.

The Small Enterprises Promotion Office (SEPO), set up at the end of 1969, was a department of the Ministry of Commerce, Industry and Mines, devoted to providing advice, guidance and training to existing and potential small entrepreneurs and handicraft producers, as well as to proposing government policies for the promotion of any aspect of non-agricultural Swazi entrepreneurship. SEPO was thus the central body around which the whole programme revolved; and it was to SEPO that the UN experts were attached. (The UN project provided for a total of nine experts, three of whom were recruited by UNIDO rather than ILO. In mid-1972, five were in post: the chief of project, experts in metalwork, ceramics, and leatherwork, and a general marketing adviser. An expert in entrepreneurial development was due to arrive in July; woodwork and handicrafts experts had still to be recruited; and recruitment of the ninth expert, in the development and use of essential oils, had been temporarily postponed.)

Following the government reorganisation, SEPO became a part of the Ministry of Industry, Mines and Tourism, and its area of responsibility was correspondingly reduced. The SEPO official and the four Peace Corps volunteers, who together had been providing an extension service for Swazi traders, were transferred to the new Ministry of Commerce and Co-operatives. SEPO is therefore now more concerned with specifically industrial or productive entrepreneurship, and the traders' advisory service in the Ministry of Commerce, for which additional local staff are to be recruited, has no formal access to the UN advisers. SEPO's directly attributable recurrent budget for 1972–73 (approved before the reorganisation) was nearly R42,000, and it will almost certainly be more expensive to operate two quite separate business promotion units. But in 1972 it seemed very unlikely that either of the Ministers concerned would accept that SEPO be made a self-governing autonomous body serving both Ministries.

The focus of the Small Enterprises Development Company (SEDCO) was less affected by the reorganisation, since its direct activities were already more concerned with industry than with commerce. SEDCO is a private limited company, registered in March 1970, in which the two main shareholders are the government (now the Ministry of Industry, Mines and Tourism) and the Swaziland Credit and Savings Bank: each of these holds 24 percent, the remaining 52 percent being reserved for private investors (principally the Swazi entrepreneurs whom the company was set up to assist). SEDCO is devoted to assembling finance for investment in small enterprises, and for providing individual entrepreneurs with facilities – such as premises and equipment – for which they are usually charged. SEDCO's small industrial estates were discussed in Chapter 5: in mid-1972, three estates, containing nearly fifty enterprises, were properly established, and their combined output had reached about R¼m per year. Two additional small Swazi enterprises had been started with SEDCO assistance at Swaziland's main (expatriate-dominated) industrial estate at Matsapha, and four other SEDCO-assisted manufacturing units were operating elsewhere. Finally, SEDCO was giving financial and technical assistance (the latter with the help of a British IVS volunteer) to a dozen Swazi contractors, employing a total of up to 450 workers, whose combined annual turnover was estimated to approach R300,000.

In its first two years, and subject to Board approval of major decisions, SEDCO was run almost entirely by the ILO 'chief of project' (technically an adviser) and one of two counterparts. These were severely overworked; several Swazi (though it is too early to confirm this) may have been encouraged to start enterprises which, although initially on a small scale so as not to incur heavy losses, were unlikely to be viable; and during the second year an ILO accountant had to be seconded to SEDCO for several months to set up a better accounting system. The author was unable, because of pressure of work on the chief of project and his acting counterpart, to obtain detailed information on which to base appraisal of SEDCO's achievements and prospects, but it was clear that SEDCO still urgently needed to strengthen its financial management and record-keeping. The chief of project was himself planning to leave Swaziland within a few weeks (though not until his replacement had been approved by the Swaziland government). Later in the year, an expatriate accountant was recruited for SEDCO from South Africa, and it seemed that the projects management, for whom a politically enforced check to SEDCO's expansion (and even a reduction in SEDCO's interests) might immediately be an advantage, would need to concentrate on reviewing and consolidating SEDCO's position.

The two remaining institutions, Swazi Craft and Amadoda Distributors, which are both concerned with assisting relatively large numbers of entrepreneurs, have been transferred to the jurisdiction of the Ministry of Commerce and Co-operatives. Swazi Craft, originally a wholly-owned subsidiary of SEDCO, is concerned with promoting handicraft production and quality, and with marketing (particularly in foreign countries). It handles about half Swaziland's total production of marketable handicrafts, and in mid-1972 its monthly purchases, which it was estimated were collected at 78 prearranged points from a total of up to 2,500 producers, had built up to about R2,000. Still operating at that stage as a subsidiary of SEDCO, it was being run by two Peace Corps volunteers and five Swazi, pending the recruitment of a UN expert; but, although it was not known how the transfer to Commerce and Co-operatives would be effected, it seemed that in the circumstances it might not be feasible for a UN handicrafts expert, answerable to SEPO, to be appointed. There were no plans for replacement of the Peace Corps volunteers, who were both due to leave later in 1972; and in view of the inexperience of the company's local staff, it also seemed doubtful whether Swazi Craft would be able to expand, or even maintain, its currently fairly limited scale of operations.

Early in 1971, SEDCO also became involved, as an equal partner with the Swazi Commercial Amadoda, in Amadoda Distributors (AD, to which reference has already been made in Chapter 3). After first tendering successfully – in straight competition with Trademarket, the European wholesaler, which at that time was 100 percent privately owned – for a contract to supply the government's grocery and cleaning material requirements, AD set up five distribution depots in different parts of the country. With effect from September 1971 it offered a wholesale service for traders. This has also been in direct competition with Trademarket, which carries a rather wider range of stock at virtually the same prices.

It is easy to see why AD should be politically important. In 1972 it already had three depots in towns not served by Trademarket; it was more prepared to sell in small lots; it was associated with the government's extension service; and Swazi traders, having always previously had to buy from foreign or expatriate concerns, set great value on having, and keeping, their own Swazi wholesaler. Nevertheless, AD has found it difficult to build up turnover. Its most eager patrons tend to be the smaller traders; the company lost just over R10,000 in its first year (ending April 1972); and in mid-1972 AD's turnover, at less than R20,000 per month, was still only 6–7 percent of Trademarket's.

By this time, negotiations had been in hand for a merger. Early in 1972 the National Industrial Development Corporation of Swaziland, another parastatal under the jurisdiction of the Ministry of Commerce,

Industry and Mines, had become part-owner of AD's competitor, by taking a 50 percent share in the private sector conglomerate of which Trademarket was a part. It seemed sensible that AD and Trademarket should merge, and the only politically acceptable formula seemed to be a reverse takeover of Trademarket by AD, though AD might not easily raise the necessary capital while, initially at least, the Trademarket management would need to be retained. When the Ministry of Commerce, Industry and Mines was split, the negotiations were frozen; and in June 1972 AD was being transferred to the Ministry of Commerce and Co-operatives. There was now a more immediate problem in the form of AD's commercial bank overdraft, of R50,000—R60,000, which had previously been guaranteed by SEDCO but which, understandably, SEDCO would not continue to guarantee if AD fell under different political and administrative direction.

Another institution closely concerned with the future of AD's overdraft is, of course, SEDCO's other main shareholder, the Swaziland Credit and Savings Bank (SCSB). The SCSB also deserves to be discussed, in the general context of Swaziland's business promotion programme, as the main source of credit to Swazi traders (which is not available to them, directly, from either AD or Trademarket). Set up in 1965, SCSB is still primarily concerned with lending to the agricultural sector. But it also has a loans scheme for housing, land and buildings, and, more significant, in 1969 it introduced a business loans scheme.

No figures are available for the breakdown of SCSB's total lending as between Africans and Europeans. It would seem, though, that the Bank is able to cover its overheads by virtue of a number of large well-secured loans to Europeans. It is this solid backing, together with the fact that, unlike an ordinary commercial bank, it is not concerned with maximising its profit, that enables it both to employ the staff necessary to appraise and administer Swazi loans and to offer such loans on reasonable terms.

SCSB's business loans scheme was discussed on Chapter 4. Most of the Swazi loans have been to traders, but a significant minority have been issued to passenger transport operators. Loans are available for any sum of R50 or more, repayable over up to five years. In the three years ending March 1972, SCSB approved a total of 127 business loans, for a total of R415,000. Numerically, the Swazi share of these loans was more than 85 percent; but the Swazi share of the total sum was considerably less than this. An interesting feature of all SCSB's lending to Swazi is that security is most commonly provided in the form of cattle: in the case of a loan to a Swazi trader, for example, the trader typically pledges beasts to the value of about two-thirds of the loan, and the difference is made up by an SCSB charge over his stocks.

Apart from the special circumstances mentioned above in connection with the distribution of the Bank's lending as between Africans and Europeans, the Swaziland Credit and Savings Bank is also outstanding, compared with comparable government banks elsewhere in Commonwealth Africa, for two significant and related features. First, the top management is still European; second, the Bank has so far resisted any attempts at political influence over its appraisal of loan applications. On the other hand, it is possible that the Bank's political immunity has in large part merely reflected the naivety and inexperience of Swazi politicians; in mid-1972 the position of SCSB Chairman passed from an expatriate to an African and there were signs that the SCSB Board, which now contained 50 percent African representation, might move towards commercially riskier policies in order to increase the Bank's lending to Swazi. In the medium to long term, this could affect the Bank's ability to raise additional capital abroad.

A number of training courses have been run for Swazi entrepreneurs, on a largely *ad hoc* basis, by SEPO. Otherwise, there is no institution in Swaziland explicitly designed to provide Swazi entrepreneurs with either managerial or technical training. School educational curricula have had a rather academic orientation, and Swazi with academic qualifications have so far had little difficulty in finding paid employment.

Curricula at some secondary schools are being diversified, however, through the introduction of more practical subjects. The Swaziland Industrial Training Institute, initially a basic trade school, has also been much expanded in recent years to provide a fairly wide range of artisan and technician courses, mainly in light engineering, and there is a Staff Training Institute, largely geared to meeting the non-technical needs of the public service.

The University of Botswana, Lesotho and Swaziland, which is based in Lesotho but is pursuing a policy of partial devolution to Botswana and Swaziland, offers a four-year Bachelor of Commerce degree. In mid-1972 the University Council was considering whether to set up polytechnic facilities in each of the three countries. It would be important to ensure, in Swaziland, that these did not unnecessarily duplicate training capacity already available at the Industrial Training Institute (which would almost certainly not itself be developed into a polytechnic, owing mainly to its geographical location). But a

Swaziland polytechnic would at least be able to provide basic commercial training of a sort not currently available.

Expatriate Companies

Swaziland's two commercial banks, Barclays and Standard, are both expatriate-owned. By reason of Swaziland's membership of the Rand area, these are effectively run as individual large branches within South Africa, despite the somewhat different exchange controls which apply in Swaziland and although some staff are directly seconded from Britain. Both banks have long tended to maintain a level of advances which would not be justified, in a closed system, by the volume of local deposits. In December 1971 total advances (including lending by SCSB) were R25.1m, compared to total deposits of R26.9m.

Although they have given useful overdraft support to SEDCO, Amadoda Distributors, and Swazi Craft, neither bank is yet much involved in direct lending to African businessmen. It is claimed, however, that despite high levels of associated bad debt, such lending is increasing as Africans become better disciplined in the management of their accounts. The government would naturally like the banks to increase their African lending rather faster, and it might be possible (though this is apparently not yet envisaged) to introduce some form of guarantee for commercial bank loans extended to Swazi entrepreneurs recommended by SEDCO or (even if this became a quite separate company) Amadoda Distributors. But both these companies would first need to put their own financial management on a more secure footing.

Except for some of the largest projects, owned by the Commonwealth Development Corporation (CDC) and a few private British companies, most of Swaziland's expatriate private sector is directly answerable to South Africa. This is not conducive to enlightened policies towards African entrepreneurs, and although CDC has approached SEDCO about the possibility of establishing a SEDCO estate near the Swazi smallholder settlement project on the Swaziland Irrigation Scheme, expatriate companies operating in Swaziland have so far done very little to help Swazi businessmen. The oil companies have given the usual forms of assistance to Swazi service station operators, but many of the largest service stations are European-owned. Generally, the expatriate companies' most important direct distribution channels, excepting Amadoda Distributors, are virtually all still owned or run by Europeans.

Conclusion

Even with access to fuller information, it would be too early to attempt a detailed evaluation of Swaziland's business promotion programme, and the future is so uncertain that any judgement is liable to be overtaken by events. SEPO (together with its commercial arm SEDCO) has certainly been remarkably successful in getting things started. The speed with which SEPO's activities were developed was quite exceptional by normal African standards. But in large part this reflected the energy and enthusiasm of two men – the first ILO chief of project, who left Swaziland at the end of July 1972 to take up an appointment in Botswana, and the then Minister of Commerce, Industry and Mines, who recognised the programme's potential and who, during 1968–72, was on the crest of a political wave which made it fairly easy to obtain Cabinet approval of his proposals. (It should also be repeated that the programme could never have been realised without substantial financial and technical assistance, from Britain and the United States as well as from UNDP.)

Especially in such a small country, there were obvious advantages – in the interests of co-ordination and of administrative economy – in giving overall responsibility for the programme to a single government agency. On the other hand, SEPO was seriously understaffed. Some of its schemes owed more to initially self-justifying optimism than to objective feasibility study (which might have betrayed potential longer-term weaknesses). And although the current UNDP support is due to be withdrawn in February 1975, it is most improbable that Swazi staff will by then be in a position to run SEPO themselves, without continued technical assistance. Furthermore, the cohesion of the programme was destroyed by the 1972 rearrangement of ministerial portfolios. This setback was not irreversible, and in principle SEPO could have been given status which enabled it to serve the Ministry of Commerce and Co-operatives as well as the Ministry of Industry, Mines and Tourism. But given the political personalities and antipathies involved, the immediate prospects were bleak – particularly, (if these were now to be quite separated from SEPO/SEDCO and the UNDP project) for Amadoda Distributors, the traders extension service, and Swazi Craft. It was likely that some Peace Corps support, at least for the traders extension service, would be maintained, but the new Ministry's leadership and administrative capacity was dubious, pending the appointment of staff.

So far as SEPO/SEDCO was concerned, the most urgent task was to review and consolidate SEDCO's existing investments. Doubts were expressed in Chapter 5 concerning the economic justification for SEDCO's main line of activity, the operation of African industrial estates; but the Swaziland estates are at least being constructed and equipped on a fairly modest scale, and they have undoubtedly demonstrated – not least importantly to the Swazi themselves – that Africans in Swaziland are capable of running successful businesses. Despite the prospect that one new SEDCO investment – an oil plant, using waste matter from the Usutu pulp mill, which was expected to go into production in August 1972 – might generate an annual net income of R30,000–R40,000, further expansion by SEDCO would need to be largely based on additional capital assistance from abroad. In this regard, it would be rash to assume, on the basis of the undoubted profitability of a few of the entrepreneurs operating on SEDCO's two main estates, that entrepeneurs in other estates, in less favoured locations, would be equally successful.

Finally, it should be emphasised that there are a number of extraneous factors, such as the European domination of the cash economy, the relative scale of Swaziland's tourist industry, and the country's geographical position and associated prospect of large sales within the customs area of, for example, artificial flowers, which together set Swaziland apart from other countries included in this study. (Botswana and Lesotho are more nearly comparable to Swaziland; but even these countries do not have such a large and regular inflow of South African tourists, eager to buy the handicrafts and clothing produced at SEDCO's estate in the Swaziland capital, Mbabane.) Because of these special factors, and also because at least in its first two years the Swaziland programme was relatively free from the political biases which would operate more strongly in most other countries (for example, in the selection of entrepreneurs), it would not be possible – even on the basis of a more rigorous appraisal of the Swaziland experience over a longer period – to forecast the probable impact of similar programmes elsewhere.

Notes

1. *Post-Independence Development Plan*, Mbabane, July 1969.

Chapter 10   **Conclusions**

The most obvious conclusion to be drawn from the present study is that, in any African country, an active programme of business promotion must be tailored to the political and other realities of the relevant local environment and, also, that assistance to entrepreneurs must be planned and administered within the context of the development policy of the specific government concerned. This does not, of course, imply that the various government programmes of African business promotion adopted in different countries over the past few years do not have much in common; and three outstanding characteristics, each of which pertain to at least the majority of the programmes which have been described, may be identified.

Characteristics of Existing Business Assistance Programmes

First, and most obviously, all the programmes involved a degree of nationalistic or political bias, in their design or in their administration, which has caused normal economic criteria to be compromised, subordinated, or even ignored. Thus, although in some cases of discrimination it may reasonably be argued that an economic loss may be outweighed by longer-term benefits, or that social considerations are overriding, there has been little attempt to appraise these prospective benefits, economic or social, and most programmes have merely represented an implicit compromise between what the government felt it could afford and what it felt, politically, it would like to do.

Second, a common shortcoming of virtually all programmes of assistance to African entrepreneurs is a lack of information, planning, and co-ordination. In this respect, the Swaziland programme has admittedly so far been exceptional; but, both because the country was so small and also because it possessed so few African entrepreneurs, it was relatively easy, given expatriate technical assistance, to ascertain the possibilities and design a realistic programme. (In mid-1972 the administration of the Swaziland programme was also still virtually immune from political influence; but by that time, as we have seen, the future of the programme was clouded with uncertainty.)

106

Finally, with the possible exception of ICDC's loan schemes, a striking characteristic of the few programmes more clearly aimed at achieving economic results is that these all rely on a substantial input of technical assistance, which tends to be concentrated on relatively small groups of entrepreneurs. This applies both to the industrial estates programmes in Kenya and Swaziland (to the extent that these are conceived in economic rather than socio-political terms) and also the Ghanaian Business Bureau and to the Partnership for Productivity project in Western Kenya. As a corollary, programmes of active business promotion — those, in other words, that involve more than relatively passive discriminatory measures in favour of Africans — have so far barely scratched the surface of the problem. Unless such programmes produce an important multiplier effect, either through their direct economic impact or by their example, the effort in any particular country must be greatly expanded if it is to have an early and significant influence on the position of the African private sector in its national economic context. Subject, again, to the partial exception of Swaziland (on account of its small size and its geographical position), we are presented with the paradox that, on their present scale, active programmes of assistance are so concentrated that they can produce only strictly localised benefits.

Possibilities for New or Improved Government Initiatives: the Scope for External Aid

In the three larger countries, it is unlikely that any of the governments (even Kenya's) would currently be prepared to sponsor a really ambitious national programme. So far, instead of devoting substantial financial and technical resources to direct entrepreneurial promotion, governments have mainly been concerned to relieve the principal external constraint to African business development, imposed by the presence of entrenched alien communities. In view of their previous dominance, some discrimination against aliens was almost inevitably regarded as a precondition to the significant improvement of African businessmen's prospects. Discrimination may also have the advantage that, compared to a more positive and specific promotion programme, it automatically favours the most enterprising African businessmen. This advantage can easily be undermined, however, by government influence over the reallocation of licences, or by the favours granted to particular businessmen by national trading corporations, and it is important to understand the main reason why governments have pursued discrimination at all. In Ghana, Kenya, and Malawi, discriminatory policies appear to have owed as much to xenophobic prejudice and to their prospective political popularity, as to any real wish to foster indigenous entrepreneurship outside the government élite. The fact that governments appear to have recognised the main external constraint to African business enterprise does not, even when they claim credit for their actions in these terms, imply that they genuinely desire the growth of an independent African middle class.

On the other hand, irrespective of their precise contemporary standpoint, some African governments may already be becoming more definitely committed to indigenous private entrepreneurship for its own sake. Kenya, for example, is acutely conscious of the growing need for new opportunities of employment. In other countries as well as Kenya, although the first post-independence priority was political consolidation (a process which is by no means completed), continued popular support increasingly depends on economic prosperity, and even where the agricultural sector continues to dominate, the improvement of rural living standards requires *inter alia* the efficient distribution of consumer goods and services. Governments might prefer to take on this responsibility themselves; but the necessary organisation and flexibility would almost certainly be beyond their administrative capacity. It can therefore be expected, particularly where (as in Malawi) the artificial gaps created by discriminatory measures are not satisfactorily filled, that there will be increasing political acceptance of the need for more active assistance to private enterprise – albeit, initially, at the lowest level, where individual entrepreneurs are too small and too diffuse to represent a significant counterweight to the government's authority.

Any government seeking to develop the African private sector first needs to collect better information about the scale and nature of existing African businesses; and it must identify the main areas of activity to be encouraged. Even where a government is principally relying on discriminatory measures, it should have some grounds for believing that local entrepreneurs are capable of taking advantage of the opportunities created for them. Moreover, although the present state of entrepreneurship varies widely from one country to another, it must not be expected that, even with the impetus which can be provided (and from time to time reinforced) through discrimination, the pace of entrepreneurial development can be very rapidly accelerated. The relatively advanced countries owe their present advantage to a multitude of historical and sociological factors. But, in Ghana as well as in Malawi or Swaziland, there remain sizeable constraints associated with long-standing local traditions and ways of life: the relief of these probably depends, most importantly, on further review of education and training curricula, and on methods of teaching.

More immediately, the pace of change crucially depends, at all levels, on the business environment. Much the most important determinant of African business development, in any country, is the general rate of economic advance; and this, though it may be reinforced by successful African entrepreneurship, is still itself largely determined by extraneous factors — such as agricultural production and prices on world commodity markets — which, obviously. the government values for more direct reasons than their effect on business opportunities. At the same time, there are ways, other than discriminatory measures, in which a government can significantly influence the business environment more directly. An early priority is to examine statutory and other regulations concerning business standards and practices to see whether requirements — for example, licensing fees or factory legislation — are unnecessarily harsh. Where the activities of entrepreneurs (likely to be relatively large ones) are affected by the day-to-day co-operation they receive from civil servants, it is obviously desirable that the latter should be not only loyal, but also genuinely sympathetic, towards the government's policy.

A government will probably find it can substantially improve the business environment at negligible cost. But a more active programme to assist African business will be much more expensive. Whereas commissions, loan charges and dividends may permit government participation in larger-scale private ventures, or the mere provision of advisory and other services, to be commercially viable or even profitable, any commitment to assist African businessmen — given the small scale on which most of these are currently operating — implies a sizeable official subsidy (such as has long been supplied to African farmers through government agricultural programmes).

Subject to a government's readiness to commit the necessary resources, the African businessman stands to benefit, in varying proportions according to the nature of his enterprise and to his own experience and capacities, from a wide range of services. For a start, a government agency or corporation, suitably staffed, may be in a better position to identify possible business opportunities and conduct appropriate feasibility studies: for example, governments may more easily see possibilities for import substitution, and assess whether local entrepreneurial capacity exists for import-substituting production. Such an agency can also offer training and advice – both in general management, including record-keeping, and in relevant technical skills. It can assist African businessmen to establish and strengthen business relationships, both with one another and with the broader business community. Much more attention could usefully be paid to maximising the stimulus to the indigenous business community, through backward and forward linkages, from the activities of predominantly state- or foreign-owned enterprises in the modern sector. Finally, provided that it can ensure sufficient supervision and follow-up, the government can directly or indirectly facilitate the African businessman's access to capital.

We have seen that government promotion of African business has tended, mistakenly, to adopt rather different priorities, seeking first to provide African businessmen with finance. It is partly the disappointing performance of African loans programmes that has induced governments (as well as expatriate advisers) to appreciate that finance should only be offered, if at all, as part of a co-ordinated assistance 'package'. It was partly on this basis that Kenya and Swaziland have experimented with promotion of African industry on specially constructed estates. But while this approach has obvious administrative as well as political advantages, equivalent resources might have been more usefully deployed in a less concentrated programme. Swaziland may, admittedly, have been able to afford the relative luxury of this approach, but the entrepreneurs on SEDCO's estates were in any case a less disproportionately favoured elite than those on KIE's first estate in Nairobi, and SEDCO's staff, including its technical specialists, were members of a single team concerned with all aspects of small enterprise development.

It follows, from the nature of commercial and industrial services (as well as the construction industry), that these *must* be assisted, if at all, on a more extensive basis. Since so many of the services required by different sorts of African businessmen can be supplied through the same individual advisers (so long as they know where to obtain additional specialist assistance if necessary), it seems better at present that all aspects of small business promotion should be concentrated, in any particular location, through a single agency or 'small business administration' (SBA). Indeed, this is a pattern which is already beginning to emerge – at least in Ghana, Kenya, and Swaziland; and it need hardly be repeated that no SBA, able to provide the regular extension service which some entrepreneurs may initially require, can be expected to be financially self-supporting. In large urban areas, there may be a case for some degree of specialisation; so that it may, for example, be better for Kenya's National Construction Corporation to remain a largely autonomous body. But even NCC could usefully draw on ICDC (if this body were re-shaped along the lines envisaged in Chapter 7) for financial services, and also, particularly for Kenyan construction firms in areas outside Nairobi where ICDC was locally represented, for advisers in general management.

It is an open question whether an SBA should have autonomous authority to make loans or give credit. If it does itself have power to lend, this may cause entrepreneurs to take a distorted view of the SBA's functions. In any case, an SBA should maintain the closest relationships with other lending agencies, and wherever possible, once it is satisfied that an individual entrepreneur can use additional capital profitably, should help him to obtain this from commercial banks.

So far as its extension service is concerned, an SBA may be likened to an agricultural promotion agency, except that agricultural services are normally primarily concerned with *technical* aspects of a form of entrepreneurship which is already a part of the entrepreneur's traditional way of life. A business extension service, which must seek to identify and develop less familiar entrepreneurial outlets, necessarily faces a more complicated task. It is difficult to make more definite recommendations as to how it should operate, both because there is so little experience in this field and because precise needs in any particular situation will vary according to the present state of African business enterprises. In Kumasi, the Ghana Business Bureau was probably deploying its resources most usefully by concentrating on assistance to directly productive enterprises, whereas an extension service in Malawi would necessarily, at first, be much involved in advice to traders. It should be added, however, that quite apart from its capacity to make a wider sectoral contribution, a business extension service also possesses the advantage of flexibility — especially valuable in the sense that it is never committed to assisting one particular group of entrepreneurs. Some element of selection will certainly be necessary, but, in contrast to the choosing of entrepreneurs for installation on an industrial estate, this can be a continuous and less binding process. It is also correspondingly easier for a well-run extension service to function towards any particular enterprise, more as a catalyst, and less as a basic input on which the entrepreneur concerned relies, indefinitely, for regular support.

Even the concept of a business extension service is a fairly new phenomenon in English-speaking Africa; and hardly any research has been done into the scale of effort required – particularly in terms of manpower resources – to identify, and adequately cover, the most promising entrepreneurs in a given area. It was suggested in Chapter 3 that, in order to achieve a coverage merely of African traders, comparable to that already being achieved in Swaziland, Malawi's Import and Export Company would need at least thirty trained extension officers, while Kenya might require more than a hundred, and the numbers would be correspondingly greater (and would need to be backed by appropriate specialists) if service and manufacturing industries were to be covered as well. The Ghana Business Bureau and the Partnership for Productivity project have been the only other experiments in this field, but it is significant that both these, like the traders' advisory service in Swaziland, were heavily dependent on external assistance. In Ghana, Kenya, or Malawi, any attempt to establish a substantial advisory service would be impossible without a large measure of external support. Even if, ideally, foreign technical assistance should ultimately aim to achieve a multiplier effect, by concentrating on training local extension officers instead of directly assisting African entrepreneurs, the training process, which would need to have a strong practical orientation, would itself involve a large measure of direct advice and assistance.

At present, it is premature to talk of African business extension services on this scale. Governments have generally not indicated that they would wish to devote such a large effort to African business promotion, and in only a few countries (including, perhaps, Lesotho and Botswana) would an externally-aided, nation-wide extension service not seem, at least at first, to take a disproportionate share of the total volume of foreign technical assistance currently being received.

Three further reservations should also be noted. First, aid donors, even if they wanted to, would find it very difficult to make sufficient numbers of suitable people available, particularly if more than one or two countries sought assistance at the same time. To some extent, and subject to fairly close supervision, the necessary work could be done by appropriately qualified volunteers: Swaziland's experience suggests that newly-qualified business studies graduates can successfully advise ordinary traders. But for more sophisticated enterprises, such as now exist in Kenya as well as in Ghana, business advisers must almost certainly have rather wider experience. At this level, although it may be relatively easy to recruit technical specialists (including economists for work on feasibility studies), the most useful general consultants probably need, at first, to be recruited direct from the private sector. A few suitable people may be available because of early retirement, but the necessary mixture of energy, flexibility, and idealism is more likely to be found in rather younger people, who will normally be reluctant to interrupt their own careers. For those still working, it might be impossible to offer terms which did not involve significant overall financial sacrifice.

Aid donors would probably themselves need to employ appropriate advisers on their headquarters staff. Alternatively or additionally, by financing short-term technical assistance assignments, they might encourage specialisation, in the general subject of entrepreneurship in developing countries, and particularly in the organisation and running of SBA's, among international business consultants. In any case present methods of technical assistance recruitment would almost certainly need to be carefully reviewed, if there were to be any chance of supplying sufficient numbers of experienced and competent advisers. For African fieldwork it would also be necessary, at least in Britain, to broaden the channels for recruitment of volunteers, and, in order to attract recently qualified technicians, it might be essential, albeit at the risk of violating traditional concepts of voluntarism, to provide much improved terms.

Furthermore, it must be appreciated that, even if, in any country, sufficient technical assistance was made available to allow a really ambitious business advisory service to be instituted, the corps of expatriate advisers would inevitably be regarded, in some quarters, as a powerful and potentially disruptive neo-colonialist force. Western businessmen inevitably import certain of their own prejudices and values. Since, as we have seen, African businessmen are operating in a cultural environment very different from that in the West, it would be wise, at a time when other expatriate 'experts' are becoming increasingly specialised in technical and relatively non-controversial skills, for any prospective aid donor to enter this field with some caution. It may be better, for both sides, that the expatriate staff of a business extension service be drawn from a number of different donor countries. Current developments in Kenya are consistent with this; but it should be repeated that not even in Kenya had the government, in mid-1972, committed itself to a co-ordinated approach towards different promotion activities.

Third, it was not possible, in the course of this study, to collect sufficient information, either about existing experiments in business extension or about other approaches such as industrial estate programmes, to permit the comparative economic evaluation of different types of programme or the broader comparison of prospective benefits with those which might be obtained from other government development expenditures. Much of the relevant data clearly did not exist; and, unless the study had been given a different status by agreement with the governments in the countries concerned, additional field research would only marginally have improved the quality of data collected. Purely from the economic point of view, it is therefore desirable that external agencies, before committing substantial resources to the direct assistance of African business promotion, study existing programmes and finance further experiments (such as, for example, the Partnership for Productivity project in Kenya). This applies both to the staffing of business extension services and to other forms of assistance.

The prospective scope for financial aid, at least while it is not closely associated with technical assistance, is currently therefore rather limited. Subject to the reservations noted above, financial assistance may be made available for the establishment or operation of SBAs, extension centres, or industrial estates. This might include the indirect provision, through these institutions, of financial assistance to individual African businessmen, but in this case the aid donor would need to be wary of undue political interference in appraisal and allocation procedures. In some countries, principally in West Africa, a few African businessmen are also now large enough to seek equity or loan finance from large-scale industrial and commercial finance corporations, most of which — such as Ghana's National Investment Bank — have already received general support from external aid agencies. At present, however, for African businessmen in most countries, a more promising approach might be to subscribe to a capital fund which would permit the government to offer a partial guarantee of credits granted by commercial banks. With all schemes to provide finance to individual businessmen, it would be necessary to ensure that the intermediate lending agency was able to provide, or call upon, an adequate follow-up facility.

It is highly desirable, and perhaps essential, that financial aid in this field should not be tied to procurement of goods or services from the donor country. Technical assistance apart, it would be impossible to tie a significant proportion of any aid given to support the recurrent cost of running an SBA, and it would be impracticable to tie a subscription to a credit guarantee fund. Some other forms of aid would merely be much more useful if they were readily available for local expenditures: trying could all too easily encourage over-capitalisation, both within individual enterprises and with respect to machinery and equipment used for common services or demonstration.

Generally, one must conclude that official aid agencies should not expect to be able to make a large and widespread direct contribution to African business promotion in the near future. In part, this reflects the apparent priorities of African governments, who would be unlikely to welcome substantial aid of this sort unless it was additional to aid they were already receiving (or expecting to receive): at least with the bigger and longer-established donors, including Britain, aid for entrepreneurship would imply correspondingly less aid for other purposes. Furthermore, it would be difficult, and perhaps politically unwise, to mount a large-scale technical assistance effort; financial support, on the other hand, would need to be largely untied and, particularly in the absence of associated technical assistance, might easily be misdirected. Above all, there is insufficient experience of the economic benefits, even in the best of circumstances, to justify a substantial input of aid resources.

There are, however, several ways in which aid donors can assist African entrepreneurial development less directly, or on an initially less ambitious scale. Some of these still depend on appropriate requests from African governments. In particular, expatriate advisers can play an important part in research, evaluation, and planning. Admittedly, some more advanced African countries may have reached a stage where local statisticians, economists and sociologists can satisfactorily do this work themselves, subject only to its being given sufficient government priority. In other countries, foreign technical assistance may be essential, even for the planning, and perhaps the implementation, of basic surveys to discover more about existing entrepreneurs and their problems. The broad experience of a foreign expert may also be invaluable to a critical appraisal of the current business environment and its effects on the activities and opportunities of all African entrepreneurs, including the great number of individually insignificant artisans and tradesmen who, with their employees, already represent an important, if largely unidentified, proportion of the employed non-agricultural labour force. Moreover, any country is more likely to attempt a proper evaluation of existing business promotion programmes, if foreign technical assistance allows this to be done fairly cheaply. In the absence of such evaluation (which, more than some of the basic survey work, *must* be done in close co-operation with the local government, with full access to available records and documents as well as to responsible officials), future planning will incorporate an unneccessary amount of ill-informed guesswork. Finally, expatriate advisers, so long as they are not operating in isolation from the local political and cultural environment, can certainly be valuable in the planning of future programmes, and if they are involved from the start, that external support is more likely to be attracted for such programmes' implementation.

Although the most valuable form of entrepreneurial training can probably be provided through an extension service, centralised institutions for managerial or technical training may also have an important bearing on entrepreneurial development, at least to the extent that these impart basic knowledge and skills. Many such institutions rely on foreign aid, both for initial construction and equipment and for staffing, and although most are only incidentally concerned (if at all) with training existing or prospective entrepreneurs rather than professional managers or technicians, two institutions, the Kenya Industrial Training Institute (still receiving technical assistance from Japan) and Uganda's ILO-sponsored Management Training and Advisory Centre, have the training of African entrepreneurs as a specific objective. The achievement motivation approach employed, for all its courses, at the Uganda Centre (see Chapter 2) might usefully be incorporated into courses run by other management training institutions, but KITI, with its exclusive commitment to running one-year courses to prepare people for self-employment, is an even more interesting experiment, which might be copied by other countries and which would probably require external support.

External official agencies can also make a useful indirect contribution without specific request from any African government. It is hoped that the present study falls into this category, at least to the extent that it gives (and has already given) wider publicity to some of the approaches being adopted in different parts of Africa and promotes better understanding of the political context of African private sector development. Much research remains to be done, however, and some of this, building on the groundwork established by de Wilde's World Bank study, needs to narrow the unnaturally wide gaps currently existing between English- and French-speaking countries. It may be that, as a result of different historical and cultural associations, English- and French-speaking countries can profit from one another's experience even less readily than, say, Malawi can from Ghana's. This especially applies to the design of appropriate institutions, and to the prospective role of direct external assistance. Nevertheless, particularly since Britain will soon be contributing to the European Development Fund, more comparisons need to be made, while there are certain fields, most notably technology, which are relatively unaffected by cultural barriers.

Most of the recent discussions about labour-intensive technology have centred, naturally, on the subject of job creation. There is no evidence, yet, that this sort of technology contributes to the development of entrepreneurship, and its use may complicate the task of management. Nevertheless, a relatively labour-intensive industry may require smaller total starting capital, and there is also the great advantage that there will probably be more flexibility in the scale of operation, so that the entrepreneur can relate the expansion of his business to the growth both of his market and of his managerial and financial capacities. Britain's Intermediate Technology Development Group is one body which already seeks to promote the development and adoption of more appropriate technologies throughout the developing world. Increased efforts of this sort, involving further basic research but also exploring and publicising the experience of other continents (particularly Asia), can assist in the sounder long-term development of African industries (privately or publicly owned), using labour-intensive equipment which can more easily be made and maintained by Africans, and which can thus enable African countries to move a little further towards economic independence.

We have seen that, notwithstanding the penchant of some African governments for nationalisation, African industries are currently still predominantly foreign-owned, and this study would not be complete without a further reference to the general role, in African private sector development, of expatriate companies. Broadly, it must be repeated that one cannot realistically expect a foreign-owned company to take unilateral steps to assist African businessmen, unless these are judged to be of some immediate or longer-term benefit to the company's activities in the country concerned. The expatriate private sector is already of some importance, however, both for the credit and training which it provides and for its purchase of locally-produced goods and services. Ironically, some foreign companies have apparently had to restrict their efforts to train African distributors, because government pressure to localise their own staff has forced them to concentrate on internal training and has also, at least in the short term, left them with fewer competent staff. On the other hand, if African governments should become more interested in building up their own business extension services, these expatriate companies could be a particularly valuable source of appropriately experienced personnel.

Main Recommendations

1. African private enterprise must play an important part in providing new employment opportunities.

2. Individual governments need to be better informed about existing African enterprise and about the influence of the existing business environment.

3. An active programme of assistance to small businessmen cannot be self-financing; the most promising way of giving assistance is through a business extension service.

4. In most African countries, an extension service working on any significant scale would initially require external support. However, some governments would currently welcome large amounts of foreign aid for this purpose only if such aid was additional to what they would otherwise expect to receive.

5. Although donor countries might have difficulty in recruiting personnel, there is greater need for technical assistance than for financial aid.

6. Any financial assistance would need to be available for local procurement.

7. There are opportunities for less direct forms of external assistance to African business development: notably, in research and surveys, evaluation of existing programmes of assistance, and planning. Some research – e.g. into industrial technologies – may even be carried out without specific request from African governments.

Glossary

AD	Amadoda Distributors
BfD	Building for Development
BPAC	Business Promotion and Advisory Centre
CDC	Commonwealth Development Corporation
DANIDA	Danish International Development Agency
DFU	Development Financing Unit (of Ghana Commercial Bank)
GBB	Ghanaian Business Bureau
GBPA	Ghanaian Business (Promotion) Act
GNTC	Ghana National Trading Corporation
ICDC	Industrial and Commercial Development Corporation
IECM	Import and Export Company of Malawi
ILO	International Labour Office
ITDG	Intermediate Technology Development Group
IVS	International Voluntary Service
KfW	Kreditanstalt für Wiederaufbau
KIE	Kenya Industrial Estates
KITI	Kenya Industrial Training Institute
KNTC	Kenya National Trading Corporation
MDC	Malawi Development Corporation
MDPI	Management Development and Productivity Institute
MTAC	Management Training and Advisory Centre
NCC	National Construction Corporation
NIB	National Investment Bank
NIVTC	National Industrial and Vocational Training Centre
NLC	National Liberation Council
NORAD	Norwegian Agency for International Development
NRC	National Redemption Council NTC
NTC	National Trading Company
OBP	Office of Business Promotion
PfP	Partnership for Productivity
RIDC	Rural Industrial Development Centre
RIDP	Rural Industrial Development Programme
RTSS	Rural Trade School, Salima
SBA	Small Business Administration
SCSB	Swaziland Credit and Savings Bank

SEDCO	Small Enterprises Development Company
SEPO	Small Enterprise Promotion Office
SRDP	Special Rural Development Programme
UNDP	United Nations Development Programme
UNIDO	United Nations Industrial Development Organisation
USAID	Unites States Agency for International Development
VP	Village Polytechnic

Index

Acheampong, Colonel, 51
African Businessmen's Association, 25, 85, 93
African Loans Board (Malawi), 87
Agricultural Development and Marketing Corporation (Malawi), 91
AID, 59, 78
Amadoda Distributors (AD), Swaziland, 27, 98-101, 103-4

Banda, Dr., 86
Bank of Ghana, 22, 60-1
Barclays Bank International, 59, 79, 91, 103
Booker McConnell, 25-6, 87-8, 92
Botswana, 17, 21, 95, 102, 104-5, 112
British Volunteer Programme, 58
Building for Development project (ITDG) 17, 73
Busia, Dr., 51-2, 54-6
Business Licensing Act (Malawi), 88
Business Promotion and Advisory Centre (BPAC), 70

Central Bank, Kenya, 79
Central Loans Board (Malawi), 87
Cocoa Purchasing Company, 55
Commercial Bank of Malawi, 91
Commonwealth Development Corporation (CDC), 103

DANIDA, 75
Denmark, 18
Development Financing Unit (DFU), Ghana Commercial Bank, 62
Development Plan, 1970-4 (Kenya), 46, 66, 79
Development Services Institute (NIB), 59

East African Community, 65
Economic Planning Division (Office of the President & Cabinet), 94
Economic Report, 1972 (Malawi), 24, 31, 84
European Development Fund, 116

de Wilde, J.C., Report on *The Development of African Private Enterprise,* 12, 15, 19, 116
District Joint Loan Boards (Kenya), 68-9, 77
District Trade Licensing Committees (Kenya), 24

Garlick, Peter, *African Traders and Economic Development in Ghana,* 8, 11, 51, 64
Germany (West), 17-18, 40-1, 45, 91
Ghana, 4-6, 8, 10, 12-14, 17-18, 21-6, 28, 30, 32-4, 38-9, 51-64, 80, 108, 110, 112, 116
Ghanaian Business Bureau (GBB), 16, 18, 55-8, 63, 107, 111-12
Ghanaian Business (Promotion) Act (1970), (GBPA), 21-2, 26, 52-6, 60
Ghana Commercial Bank, 59, 61-2
Ghanaian Enterprises Advisory Committee, 21-2, 52, 55-6
Ghanaian Enterprises Decree (1968), 21, 55
Ghana Guarantee Corporation, 55
Ghana National Trading Corporation (GNTC), 26, 28, 31, 52-4, 62
Ghana Post Office Savings Bank, 59

Hameed, K.A. *Some Aspects of the Emergence of Entrepreneurship in a Newly Independent Country,* 11

121